WALKING

IN

THE

RAIN

dept.store *for* the mind

WALKING

IN

THE

RAIN

SETTING OUT ON TWO FEET
CAN LEAD TO WONDERFUL
JOURNEYS OF THE MIND

aster

An Hachette UK Company

www.hachette.co.uk

First published in Great Britain in 2017 by Aster, a division of
Octopus Publishing Group Ltd, Carmelite House
50 Victoria Embankment, London EC4Y 0DZ
www.octopusbooks.co.uk
www.octopusbooksusa.com

Distributed in the US by Hachette Book Group
1290 Avenue of the Americas
4th and 5th Floors, New York, NY 10104

Distributed in Canada by Canadian Manda Group
664 Annette St., Toronto, Ontario, Canada M6S 2C8

ISBN 978-1-91202-317-2

A CIP catalog record for this book is available from the British Library.

Printed and bound in China

10 9 8 7 6 5 4 3 2 1

Consultant Publisher Kate Adams
Editor Pollyanna Poulter
Copy Editor Alison Wormleighton
Consultant Editor Ruth Williams
Senior Designer Jaz Bahra at Octopus
Creative Direction and Design Katie Steel and Jo Raynsford at Supafrank
Photography Libbi Pedder
Illustrator Alexandra Ethell
Production Controller Beata Kibil

dept.store *for* the mind

BEAUTIFUL WORDS FOR THE MIND

Each book offers stories and ideas about creating daily habits that are kind to the mind, whether through our connection with nature, our creativity or everyday tasks, or simply knowing and feeling more accepting of ourselves. The books stretch the mind and soul, so that we may color outside the lines, experience the moments of wonder that are right there in front of us, and occasionally venture out of our safe harbors.

deptstoreforthemind.com is the exciting new creative venture by Sophie Howarth, cofounder of the School of Life. The Department Store for the Mind is a place to explore the world inside your head: a vast and unique terrain of thoughts, ideas, emotions, and memories.

www.deptstoreforthemind.com

FOR PUCK, WHOSE LITTLE SPIRIT

WILL PLAY ON IN THE WOODS FOREVER

INTRODUCTION

Walking is medicine for the mind. It helps us slow down and think things through. It also helps us perk up and generate new ideas. There are few activities as readily available and revitalizing as a brisk walk, or as soothing and stimulating as a long walk. Wonderful things can happen when we set out on two feet.

Within these pages you will find stories from artists, designers, writers, psychologists, and speakers who are inspired by the effect of pacing outdoors. You will hear of walks in the city, hikes through woods at dawn, and epic adventures involving long journeys on foot. No matter the scale of the tale, the writer offers lessons they learned of a simple, human nature that we can all understand.

Each chapter invites you to witness a personal journey and take from it what you will. In a world where so much of the noise around us suggests we are not good enough as we are, and that we must seek to change, these accounts try to do something different. They aim instead to invite a stroll into the complex pathways of the mind to discover the beauty of our own quirky individuality.

As we get more adept at feeling good about our own funny ways, we may become more able to warm to the same in others. Through tending ourselves, we may go some way to tending our world.

In each chapter you will discover suggestions and ideas about how to create simple daily habits from the writer's thinking. Some ideas might work for you and others will pass you by. This is perfectly fine as there are enough for each reader to discover a little gem to call their own.

EAT,
SLEEP,

WALK

EAT, SLEEP, WALK

Walking is essential, every day

Katie Steel | Supafrank with Louise Ellaway | Writer

When I started the morning walks, I'm sure I looked half-mad.

I had a stick, a long gnarled-up thing that stood up to my shoulder. I was wearing a gray zip-up parka that resolutely flapped from one shoulder, no matter how many times I tried to shrug it back on. I had one pair of good leather walking boots.

And I knew, from the muted alarm in the eyes of passers-by, that I had a fearful determination on my face.

I'd just moved from the heart of London to a small village nestled among rolling and wooded hills. In the year before the move, my business partnership had gently crumbled. That, and a childhood of turmoil, had left me with a feeling of uncontrollable anxiety.

All the way through my twenties I had searched for adventure, or for escape in the disguise of progress. I traveled a lot and was totally restless. I wanted an exotic journey, I wanted a great career, and I never felt settled in any of it. There was a constant feeling that I needed to be somewhere else. To be *not* in the moment.

So many things go into a sense of self. All I knew was that by the time I'd moved away from the city, mine had reached a roiling tumult, a place where every thought had a frenetic energy. I had anxiety to the point where I would

12

" "

IT'S EASY
TO FORGET
THAT ANXIETY
IS A PHYSICAL
EXPERIENCE

wake up with butterflies each morning for many years. I'd get shortness of breath just going into work. My mind was like a balloon, filling up with air and deflating, filling and deflating again—till it was all stretched and the life was gone from it. I was totally phobic about what my life was going to be.

To make things worse, I'd just been put on strict doctor's orders to give up my most effective coping mechanism—my cigarettes.

So I took up walking.

SLOW EXPECTATIONS

The morning walk, when I began it, was 3 miles long. It was winter, and the dawn was unappealing. I'd ask my partner, Tom, to drop me off on his way to work, just to take the choice out of it. He'd boot me out of the car and leave me stranded with only my two feet to carry me. From there on, I was alone—out in the cold and often apprehensive.

> "I COULDN'T BELIEVE, AFTER COMING THIS FAR, THAT I'D LOST THAT INSTINCTIVE PART OF ME—THE PART THAT KNEW HOW TO DO THINGS BRAVELY AND SIMPLY"

My route took me on a meandering stomp through dense woodland. Even though the path led me through undergrowth, occasionally I would poke my head out between branches to emerge at a wide, expansive vista with a view right over the downs. On a clear morning I could look out from the top of a hill and see London shimmering in the distance.

From the very first week that I moved to the countryside, I took this walk each and every day. It started as a way to cope, no more and no less. I had no expectations of it. Walking was just to give some kind of structure to the days that otherwise sprawled ahead of me, as I worked from a desk at home, trying to feel out a new path for my business. And my walks provided a distraction from the yawning call of my tobacco cravings.

Over time, though, they have become my center, and my lifeline—asking only for my steady commitment, and giving back infinitely more.

EARLY ENCOUNTERS

My initial encounters with the woodland showed me just how far I'd strayed from myself.

At the beginning, it was manic. I was walking and walking, and talking in my mind, trying to frame my life to date—to work out who I was, what I was doing, and just how I'd ended up talking to myself in a field in the middle of nowhere.

Sometimes I'd stop sharp, only to realize I was singing to myself, loudly.

My nerves were never so apparent as when, on one of my early, exploratory routes, I came to a small stream. Over the stream was a simple plank bridge.

It's not that I'd never seen a stream before. As a child, I'd grown up rurally. And in truth, this was little more than a brook. I came toward it, striding boldly at my usual frantic pace. But as I drew nearer, I began to freak out.

I don't know how to get over this. I don't know how to get over this.

The voice of panic rose strongly, near overwhelming me.

After a long hesitation, I gathered myself. Who was I, to balk at the prospect of a few steps across a friendly wooden beam? I couldn't believe, after coming this far, that I'd lost that instinctive part of me—the part that knew how to do things bravely and simply. I'd lost touch with the quick, easy courage of someone at home in their natural environment, comfortable in a forest or grassland teeming with unpredictable life.

I was almost floored by the fear.

" "

I FEEL
A STRANGE
SOLIDARITY
BETWEEN THE
CHANGEABLE
SEASONS
AND MY OWN
SHIFTING
EMOTIONS

I took a deep breath, and ran across.

Other encounters called for a different kind of courage.

I carried my stick in part for company—but in part to ward off moody Highland cows, whose presence on the hills loomed large in my imagination.

Often, in those early days (before I had the company of Nell, my sheepdog), I'd walk into a field to a sense of presence. It would take a good minute or two to realize that just a short distance away, among the ferns, was a muntjac deer standing and peering out at me. We would stand there, stock still, each fixed by the other's gaze.

Things were changing, slowly, slowly.

FINDING A PACE
As I walked, I began to notice.

First I noticed the dawn. At 6 A.M., the air often has a dense, soggy smear to it—the kind of cloud cover that, from behind the protection of a window, looks oppressive.

But the moment you cross the threshold, you feel different. Out there, skin to skin with it, the cloud changes. Within the first few minutes of a walk, you feel your body adjust. Your skin puckers up with chill, or breaks into a sweat in response to the heaviness of the air.

I have gradually come to enjoy being outside more than in.

Each morning brings something new. One morning the cloud cover will thicken and the breeze will whip up, and on another morning the sun will burn off the mist and warm you. Outside, I find myself a part of the conversation. My favorite days are those where I set out in a darkish, foggy air, and the light comes up slowly, as I'm walking.

Soon, I noticed my feet. On my walk, the forest floor is spongy. In such a thick canopy, leaves fall down to make a kind of buoyant surface, a thick bed of plant matter—light, springy, and sandy beneath my feet. As I walk, my awareness sinks to the ground, and I become more and more conscious of a rhythm carrying me forward.

It's easy to forget that anxiety is a physical experience. In its darker moments, it's known for putting you "in your head" and seeming to snatch the life out of your chest, forcing your heart up into your throat.

I had grown accustomed to the feeling—not just of stress, which creates a strained relationship to the pull of time, but of the edges of terror, marked by a voiceless, panic-heavy lurching, and a mind filled to the brim with scathing self-attack. I couldn't remember how it felt to be settled and calm.

> "WITHIN THE FIRST FEW MINUTES OF
> A WALK, YOU FEEL YOUR BODY ADJUST.
> YOUR SKIN PUCKERS UP WITH CHILL,
> OR BREAKS INTO A SWEAT IN RESPONSE
> TO THE HEAVINESS OF THE AIR."

If anxiety has a rhythm, then it is the constant, uneasy pitter-patter of consciousness circling itself. I found the rhythm of my walking to be its partner, and its antidote.

My own footsteps. Steady, slow, repetitive. When I move this way, something shifts inside me.

WALKING IN THE CHANGES

The walks brought a slow-burning space for observation.

People say London is seasonless, but I think it's a matter of attention.

Walking, I began to sense the minute, gentle whispers emanating from each part of the landscape. I could hear the humming chorus that calls out the changing of a season.

My eyes became attuned to the colors. The Surrey Hills in summer are a vivid purple, thanks to fields of heather in bloom. As the seasons pass, the landscape is hit by a sweep of sudden life and demise. New arrivals spread in waves across fields I have only just got used to: a bed of buttercups rising in a plain meadow, a sprout of mushrooms emerging lurid red among wet shoots of grass.

Snowdrop. Daffodil. Bluebell.

> "A WALK DOESN'T TAKE YOU AWAY
> FROM YOUR TROUBLES. IT DRAWS
> YOU RIGHT ALONGSIDE THEM, IN THE
> SPACE AND SILENCE, TO LET THE
> QUIETER PARTS OF YOURSELF SPEAK."

As I watch these cycles unfold, I feel a strange solidarity between the changeable seasons and my own shifting emotions. Nature doesn't stay benevolent and stable all of the time. Seasons wreak havoc, whether violent or soft, but always vibrant. They bring life to a landscape.

WALKING THE TROUBLES

My walk's short pocket of time—just an hour—has taken on its own dimensions. For a space born of repetition, it never feels the same.

I have noticed that, like weather patterns passing over and around me, my own being changes and expands into this space. Sometimes I feel large and bounding and passionate. Other times I feel small and narrowed.

Some days, I wake with a crystal clarity. On others, the ferreting voices of anxiety harass me and will persist until some point mid-walk. Or they will persist all the way through and relief will only come later, as I'm sitting at the breakfast table with flushed cheeks and a body ready, finally, to pause.

The deepest and most surprising benefit is that, without having to forcibly think positively (or really think about anything), a walk will soothe me. For one hour each morning, my usual overthinking is quiet, and I am absorbed in the movement.

If there is an internal voice, it's in a different register. Maybe it's having your feet firmly planted on the ground with each step, but a walk doesn't take you away from your troubles. It draws you right alongside them, in the space and silence, to let the quieter parts of yourself speak.

WALKING HOME

I talk to myself more comfortably now. And sing! I think I'm finally at ease with it. I see it as a part of the process.

If there's a difficult conversation to have, I'll make sure I take a long walk beforehand. The time alone, pacing, is what I need to play a scenario over.

I'm not that good at knowing where I stand in situations, or in relationships. In the heat of a dynamic, it can be easy to forget yourself. I'll have discussions with people in my head, trying to figure out how to solve problems or how to explain how I feel. Often, as a result, the real-life conversations turn out more positive than if I'd had them straight off the bat. They feel more truthful.

But it's more than that. I somehow find my boundaries when I'm walking.

The walk becomes a place in itself. I'm brave enough, there, to express myself fully. By granting me time to reflect on how I feel about things, and to speak of them frankly, walking helps me remember that I'm a human, I'm a part of the world.

I can float options in my head, get to the bare bones of a situation, and start to see, actually—who I am is right here. This is what I believe in.

When a situation is taking me far away from who I am, walking will faithfully bring me home.

AN EVERYDAY REMEDY

I feel strong now. I feel like a phenomenally strong person. Oh, and I haven't smoked in six years.

If you ask me, it's all in the walking.

There's a drive, almost an anticipation—I just get up and I'm straight out the door. I call my sister sometimes, but mostly I still walk alone, except for my fractious sheepdog companion, Nell, who bounds along beside me.

I love that it doesn't take much money, or time, or a suite of special Lycra accessories. It's nothing deep or mysterious. I just have to get up a bit earlier, and get out the door.

22

I can hardly believe the change that has come from something so simple.

It's like breathing to me now. There are no ifs, no buts or maybes—no real decision to make. If it's snowy or raining, I might go for a shorter route. Sometimes I'll arrive home wet through. But I'll always do it.

Because if I don't, I won't feel like myself.

Now I head to my desk in the morning with half-wet hair and rosy cheeks, knowing that my fears have been kneaded away into the earth by the soles of my feet.

GET THE EAT, SLEEP, WALK HABIT

Ideas for making walking essential

1 | MINDSET

Check in on how you think about walking. Is it a chore? A pleasure? Just exercise? Can you challenge your thinking? Can it just be a thing that is done to keep the body's motor running?

2 | JUST OUTSIDE

How could you make the distance right for you and where you are now? Think of being just outside your comfort zone at first. Little steps will get you there more surely.

3 | DROP OFF?

Katie's boyfriend took the choice away and just dropped her off in the morning, so she had to walk back. How could you take the choice out of it? Who might help you?

4 | HAPPY HABITS

How could you create a little walking routine to get you in the mood? Can you create your own special way of getting ready? What regular reward could you have on return?

5 | ALL WEATHERS

Come sunny days, wind, drizzle, or worse, keep the pacing going. Can you notice any seasonal patterns inside you as well as in the great outside?

6 | KEEPING IT GOING

Forgive yourself if you miss a day or two, or a week or more. Can you find a new way in? Can you make the challenge a little gentler? Can you make the reward a little greater?

SIDE

SIDE BY SIDE

Conversation on the move

John-Paul Flintoff | Speak Listen

When I was 12 years old, I went for a walk that lasted the whole night. Just me and Tom Mayers. It was one of the most exciting adventures of my life.

We were Boy Scouts, from central London. Once a year, the troop drove out to the Berkshire countryside for these night hikes: given maps, and instructions to follow, we split up into groups of two or three and marched as fast as we could to our destination. The first ones to arrive, most likely sometime in the small hours of the morning, were the winners.

It was my first year, and Tom's too, but we'd been trusted to manage on our own, without an older boy to lead us.

Mind you, Tom *was* older than me—by several months, a degree of seniority that can feel significant when you are 12. What's more, I looked up to him as somebody very brave. On a previous trip outside London, he'd fearlessly climbed a cliff face, and hadn't hesitated to rappel off the top again afterward.

I might have felt intimidated by him, but Tom had a friendly smile and a self-deprecating manner. And, though willing, he was not as good as me at soccer. We were equals.

Our leader, Pete, a hero of mine, had taken great care preparing the hike, and dropped us all off in different places. When Tom and I jumped out of the Ford minivan, at a bend in a country road, it was dark already. Stars twinkled

" "

CHANGING
SOMETHING
ABOUT THE BODY
CAN CHANGE THE
WAY WE THINK

overhead. This being countryside, we could pick out the familiar shape of the constellation Orion, and we'd always be able to find north, Pete reminded us, if we looked for the North Star.

Our eyes became accustomed to the dark and we set off, into a field, staggering slightly under the weight of our backpacks, which were filled with a change of clothes, maps, compasses, sandwiches, fruit, candy bars and a thermos of hot tea. As the Ford drove away, we turned on our flashlights. We had two each.

You won't be surprised to learn that I don't remember everything. But some things do stick in the mind.

We told jokes. Pretty stupid ones, I expect.

We slashed with sticks at the plants around us.

And like the pilgrims in Chaucer's *Canterbury Tales*, we told stories. About school, mostly. Tom went to a well known private school, and I went to a notorious public school. I hated it, and felt scared there, but I told my stories with bravado, too proud to show myself as the victim. Tom seemed impressed by the unruly behavior I described, which was some consolation.

As we talked, we kept an eye on our maps, and compasses, navigating through fields, across roads, and into woods.

One moment I remember vividly. Among the trees, we shone a flashlight in each hand, and wheeled them around to scatter light everywhere. But the dancing shadows of one tree across another only frightened us more. Still holding our flashlights, we picked up large stones and lobbed them around liberally, in case anybody was hiding; but this action gave the beams of light an even more chaotic quality, and so we ran for a while, backpacks bouncing heavily on our backs, till the wood was behind us.

Coming out again, we felt some relief, but now fear had entered into us, and we started to wonder what was coming next. Was it safe to walk across fields?

What if a farmer saw us, thought we were burglars and shot us?

When we walked along roads we felt safer, until we heard a car approaching. Would it hit us? Or would the driver screech to a halt, and kidnap us?

"Are you scared?"

"Yeah—but not really."

This was reassuring. Despite his bravery on a rock face, Tom was capable of fear. He was like me.

"WALKING PROVIDES A CONTEXT
FOR CONVERSATION, AND A
DIFFERENT WAY OF DOING IT"

And we walked on, stumbling over the uneven ground in darkness after we had used up our flashlight batteries. To make sense of our maps, we had to find streetlights, which meant taking some lengthy detours. But it was late spring, and before long we had the pale light of dawn to read by, and we staggered half-asleep toward Pete and his Ford.

Even at the time, I knew the night hike was about more than just following a map and written instructions. It was some kind of rite, to test our capacity to get along. As it turned out, it would make us best friends. And I'm convinced that this was because we had a chance to talk that would never have been possible if we hadn't gone out for a walk.

Walking provides a context for conversation, and a different way of doing it.

It would have been impossible to talk the way I did with Tom if we'd been sitting across a table from each other. We certainly wouldn't have devoted such a long time to it. More than that, there's something very direct about staring into somebody's face when you are chatting. Young people especially

" "

IT'S A PLACE
OF EXCITEMENT,
AND FEAR,
OFTEN
BOTH AT ONCE

can feel awkward, when the topic is intense. Eyes slide down, and to the side. Utterances get shorter, dwindling to monosyllables.

That's certainly how I was, anyway. And I'm sorry to report that there are still times when I can become monosyllabic. It's most likely when I'm sitting at a table, feeling that I'm being lectured. After too much of that, I can't take it any more. I rise from my seat, ready to get out of there.

WHAT COMES NEXT?

Years after my night hike, I studied English literature at university, and learned about the "liminal zone," which is the outside place where writers send their characters to be changed by what happens to them there. Coined by anthropologists, the term liminal zone comes from the Latin for "threshold" and is used to describe the ambiguous space in the middle of a ritual, when participants are no longer what they were before and haven't yet become what they will soon be. It's a place of excitement, and fear, often both at once.

In storytelling, I learned, the zone is typically a wild place, such as a forest (*A Midsummer's Night's Dream*) or water (*Moby Dick*) or a combination of both (*Peter Pan*). But it can also be somewhere relatively tame (a picnic, in Jane Austen's *Emma*). As well as a place, it can describe a special interval in time, like the dream in which Jacob meets God, in Genesis, or the pause between engagement and marriage, or between death and burial. Or an everyday occurrence, like twilight.

The key thing is that people are changed by stepping into the liminal zone. And that happens a lot more often than we might think. It can happen whenever we go out for a walk with somebody.

Please give me a moment to explain.

It seemed obvious, after studying English, to become a writer. A journalist, mostly, but also an author of books, and then, as my interest in narrative developed, a theatrical improviser. It was the latter that led to me training with the impro legend Keith Johnstone.

Keith taught us a remarkable way of creating stories on the spot. He called it "What Comes Next?" The rules were very simple. Working in pairs, we came up with just one line of a story at a time. It had to start with the word "we" and it had to describe something in the present tense.

"We go for a walk..." might be one example.

After the first person has spoken that first line of the story, the second person gets to approve it. If it's something they like, they say, "Yes! What comes next?" And the storyteller continues, one line at a time.

But if the listener doesn't like a line, they say, "No!" And the storyteller and the listener then trade roles, with the person who was previously listening now making up the story, one line at a time, until such a time as the other person says no, and they change places again.

If both people are strictly honest, saying yes and no according to how they truly feel, the story will by definition be a story that pleases them both.

"WE GET TANGLED UP IN THE
INTELLECTUAL CONTENT OF
WHATEVER'S BEING DISCUSSED"

It struck me at the time that it would be a wonderful thing if the same rules could be applied to all conversations. Anybody could say yes or no, at any point, without needing to justify themselves.

Alas, that's rarely the case, because many people, by adulthood, have developed a strong need either to dominate or to be submissive in conversations. And we're not trained to trust our intuition, so instead of paying attention to what our feelings tell us about whether we even want to talk about something, we get tangled up in the intellectual content of whatever's being discussed. It takes training, and application, to overcome that.

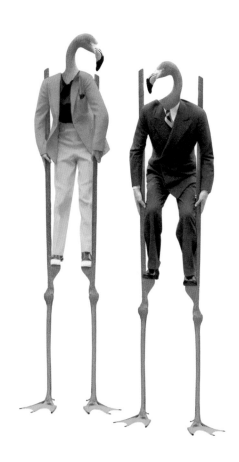

The first time I played "What Comes Next?" was with an actor from Denmark, Pernille Sørensen. I don't remember the whole story, but I remember Pernille looking really delighted by something I said (I wish I could tell you what it was), and her suggestions were spot on, too. We ended by flying an imaginary plane together, both holding imaginary steering wheels as we whizzed around the room, then up into the clouds, where we met God, before Keith stopped us.

> "PEOPLE GET STUCK, MENTALLY,
> WHEN THEY ARE PHYSICALLY STUCK.
> TO RELEASE OURSELVES, WE NEED
> ONLY TO GET UP AND MOVE."

Weirdly, I felt slightly blessed afterward. And that, I'm convinced, is because Keith insisted we didn't just make up stories in our heads. We had to enact them, and plentiful evidence suggests that if you perform something, the same parts of your brain are engaged as if you were experiencing it for real. The body, overlooked in this respect by most educational institutions, is a remarkable instrument for learning. A full immersion into a cocreated liminal zone.

MENTAL FREEDOM COMES FROM MOVEMENT

I have seen this type of learning many times, working with others to help get them past the things that hold them back. Changing something about the body can change the way we think.

Probably the most remarkable incident of this was when I was working with a woman in California. (I was in London. This took place online.)

We were both sitting down, at our desks, and the conversation was going around in circles. She couldn't get past mental obstacles that didn't, to me, seem particularly difficult. And she was getting more and more frustrated.

I asked her to see if the problem looked any different if she stood up.

She rose from her seat. Now all I could see on my computer screen was her midriff, and her hands resting on the desk.

The effect was astonishing. "Oh my God! It's a revelation!" she said. "I get it now. I totally see what the problem is."

And she spelled it out, while I watched her hands wheeling.

The ideas we have, and our capacity to process them, are intimately connected to what we do with our body. People get stuck, mentally, when they are physically stuck. To release ourselves, we need only to get up and move.

WHAT ABOUT DIFFICULT MOMENTS?

Mind you, I don't want to pretend that walking, of itself, is the solution to everything. I have been on many walks that felt truly wonderful, but walks aren't always "nice," or easy, and it would be dishonest to pretend otherwise. After raging on the blasted heath, King Lear lost his mind, and I can remember one walk on London's largest wilderness, Hampstead Heath (a liminal zone near my home), when the bad mood among my companions turned the place briefly into a corner of hell.

On that occasion, cellphone screens twinkled dimly, as angry text messages flew around. There was a disagreement with an absent texting friend that caused upset to those who were on the walk with me. This happens—I'm just as likely to be distracted by my phone as the next person. But what I remember disliking most was being with people who were distracted by phones to such a degree that they became distant. They were so preoccupied by the argument that it seemed as if they weren't really there.

Another time, I was walking with somebody in the dense traffic of Shoreditch, in central London, and listening as he outlined a number of pressing difficulties. Stuck in his head, he was oblivious to everything around us, and not just the boring, everyday aspects of the city but also surprising details that can only be noticed when you pay attention.

35

I'm not entirely sure why I said what I said next. Was my motive generous, designed to pull him back to the comfort and safety of the here and now? Or had I just had enough?

"Oh look! That's cabbage. Somebody has planted cabbage next to the sidewalk." (It was true.)

My companion glanced over, pulled a slightly irritated expression, then continued speaking as before.

I find that I do this a lot. Sometimes it annoys people and they tell me so. But not always.

BEING PRESENT

A while afterward, my companion thanked me for pulling him back to the here and now. ("I was going around in circles, and not being very present," he admitted.) So I'm giving myself permission to continue to intervene like this. After all, conversation is two-way. Just because I go for a walk with somebody doesn't mean that I want to submit myself entirely to the thing that's on their mind. Sometimes, I want to be able to notice the lost-cat poster, the buds on the magnolia, or the name on the gravestone.

GET THE SIDE-BY-SIDE HABIT

Ideas for mixing conversation and movement

1 | WALKING STORIES

What are your walking stories? How did movement play a part in your story? Can you spot something in your telling, hold onto the memory, and use it as a persuasion to try it again?

2 | CAFÉ OR PARK?

Sharing a coffee or beer is fun but could you do it after a stroll? How might a little amble together before the treat play out? When and with whom might you try it out?

3 | LIMINAL ZONE

How do you feel about encountering your own liminal zones? How might you search them out a little more, offer them a warmer welcome, and pause within for just a moment longer?

4 | INTUITIVE EARS

When sharing a conversation, what does your intuition encourage you to say when logic might not concur? What happens when you're swayed by the intuitive voice? How does the depth of connection change?

5 | MIND MOVEMENT

If your mind reaches a block and a new angle is needed, could moving your body help? Just standing up or strolling maybe? Could you take this into your conversations (particularly the tricky ones)?

6 | PRESENCE

When walking and talking together, how might the little things you notice as you pass weave themselves into the to and fro of your exchange? What happens when you do?

WILD

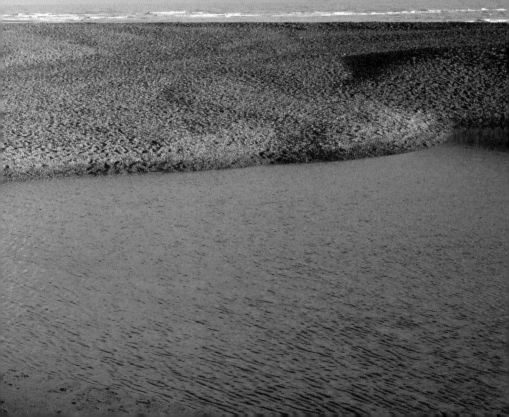

BE
AU
TY

WILD BEAUTY

Let nature be your teacher

Kate Peers | Mad about the boys

nature • noun. The phenomena of the physical world collectively, including plants, animals, the landscape, and other features and products of the earth, as opposed to humans or human creations.

A PICNIC IN THE PARK

The sun was blazing down and I had spent the day with friends in London's Regent's Park, lazing in the grass, enjoying a picnic, looking up at the blue skies, and appreciating a Saturday in the city. Then I'd gone home to get changed, before heading out for dinner, when the phone rang with news that would change my life for ever.

My mother, aged 55, was unconscious, having suffered a brain aneurysm. There was nothing that anyone could do, no brain activity. I had to find a way to get back up north to say goodbye. That same sunny day went cold and dark. Nothing outside had changed but everything inside had, and the whole world looked different.

The next few days were spent at the hospital and in my grandfather's garden across the road. The sun that I had enjoyed so much was now annoying, painful, irritating. It made me angry, especially since everyone I saw looked so happy, their endorphins boosted by the blazing heat and blue skies.

" "

THE SIMPLICITY
OF SILENCE IN
THE NATURAL
ENVIRONMENT
IS HEALING

THEN THE RAIN CAME

My mom died and then the rain came. I like to think about the rain that followed as the world in mourning for the loss of someone so special. I slipped into a trancelike state of grief and shock for some months, and it was nature that now became my source of calm. The people around me were in a different universe, and when I talked to them it felt like I was in a bubble, slightly removed from day-to-day life. But the sky stayed where it was, and the earth kept me grounded. I had lost my mother, but mother nature was the one certain thing in my life.

"THE SKY STAYED WHERE IT WAS, AND THE EARTH KEPT ME GROUNDED"

My journey through grief took me traveling, from the dinosaur-like landscape of the Galapagos Islands to the hilltops of New Zealand, from the lakes of Guatemala to deserts and walking up the mountains of the Andes. Traveling through the seasons, across different landscapes, I observed how nature could help our understanding of the circle of life.

A four-day walk across New Zealand's Abel Tasman National Park, with a tent on my back and some basic supplies, was an opportunity to focus on walking itself. The goal was to get from one side of the park to the other while camping on the way. The temptation to rush to each camping spot was inherent—we could have simply sat down and relaxed for the rest of the day, but nature gave us natural stopping points along the way. We would swim in little bays, take photos of rare flowers, and sit silently and spot birds, before continuing with our walk. It taught us patience.

FALL SILENT AND TURN UP THE VOLUME ON NATURE

The simplicity of silence in the natural environment is healing. At first when silence stretches out for longer than you are used to, a resistance, an almost itchy quality surrounding your being, creeps in. Letting this be and waiting for it to pass was worth every wriggly moment. As all that brain energy, consumed with busy chatting, is freed, it is as though it naturally redirects to the nourishment of the senses. Without anything more than slowing down and waiting, the natural world is amplified. Water sounds develop a tonal, rhythmic quality reminiscent of orchestrated music. The depth of color and impact of light and shade emerge. Scents and smells waft around, gently awakening emotional memories. The sensory amplification dulls the inner turmoil and hurt. Being beside nature and noticing gives license to just be and breathe, without the need for wordy explanations. Something inside me could begin to let go.

While in New Zealand I went on a yoga retreat at the top of a mountain in Golden Bay. For two weeks I rose at first light, did yoga before breakfast, and was silent until late morning. A practice called *mouna* (or silence) occurred from 8:30 P.M. to 8:30 A.M. each day in order to give space for the mind to turn inward and to go deeper into witnessing one's thoughts and feelings.

Again, there was something about the silence that turned up the volume on the senses. It was here that I could observe and connect with nature without disruption. The often intense yoga and breathing sessions brought my grief and tears to the surface. Taking long walks out to the waterfall nearby or helping with the gardening was healing and allowed me just to be as I was, without trying to change how I felt.

CELEBRATE RAINFALL

A drought was occurring during my stay, and we had to limit our water use to a one-minute shower a day. When I arrived there, I had negative feelings about rain. I celebrated being in the sunshine and leaving the gloomy rain back home in the UK. This drought taught me to see the rain in a different light, and to be grateful for it.

Rain bestows life on parched earth. It helps crops grow, leaving behind dirty, muddy roads and fields, only for them to restore themselves and flourish. This is similar to our beautiful lives in which we face messy situations but jump up and repair ourselves.

" "

YOU MUST TREAD
LIGHTLY AND LEAVE
LITTLE TRACE OF
YOUR PRESENCE IN
THE LANDSCAPES
THROUGH WHICH
YOU PASS

RESPECT THE OCEAN

Surfing and swimming in the ocean formed a big part of the trip. Underwater diving with sharks, giant turtles, dolphins, and manta rays is like visiting another world. We are reminded not only to think hard about what we put into the water system, but that despite the richness of the sea, we need to remain within our limits. The most important lesson for us to learn from the sea is respect for it.

The ocean teaches us that there's always another wave, even if the earlier one returns, and that there's invariably more to life, even with its setbacks. There are some things that we cannot control, and nature teaches us that we must learn to move on peacefully and not hold onto things.

BANANAS ON AN OLIVE TREE

Nature is perfectly balanced and 100 percent efficient. You never see a pear tree growing acorns, or bananas growing on an olive tree. Nature follows laws and rarely deviates from them. If it went rogue, we would be in serious trouble. A tree doesn't grow for the benefit of just the tree, it grows for the benefit of the world. Everything has a purpose.

Fields that are barren and slushy can also be green and vibrant. Reflecting the seasons perfectly, they endure plowing and weeding, feeding and watering to provide farmers with the best crops, or land for their herds. Fields teach us about the hard work that needs to go into life in order to reap rewards.

From the biting winter winds to the scorching heat from the sun, the cycles within nature reflect the cycles within us and tell us how and when to be the most productive. Nature teaches us how to survive and gives us lessons in dealing with adversity. All species depend on one another, with each of them forming an integral part of the ecology, no matter how small their contribution may seem.

Mother nature is wild, delicate, murderous, and nurturing. The feminine aspect we witness when we notice the depths of her details is not a product of spa days, high heels, or endless ironing. She makes ridiculous our attempts to control the inevitable passage of time and celebrates the necessity of death and rebirth. She draws forth our memories of being evolved from the same earth and, in some way, gives permission to our passions, fears, and mightiness, while simultaneously releasing us to notice how inconsequential our worries are against the backdrop of time. There is something in that wild woman that reassures you that it is perfectly wonderful and absolutely futile to be anything other than your true self.

Nature demands mutual respect and a deep appreciation of difference.

There is something in your being that is awakened when you learn to just be and quietly observe the natural world, something that says you must tread lightly and leave little trace of your presence in the landscapes through which you pass. We follow these ideas of sustainability now through social media, purchasing decisions, marketing campaigns, and business strategy. Mother nature always knew; we had just stopped listening to her for a century or so.

"MOTHER NATURE ALWAYS KNEW;
WE HAD JUST STOPPED LISTENING
TO HER FOR A CENTURY OR SO"

WISDOM BEGINS IN WONDER

The minute that children can walk, they explore the outdoors with glee and joy, spotting floating clouds, blooming flowers, twinkling stars, and falling leaves. On a walk, they stop and observe the elements around them, collecting sticks and leaves and picking flowers as they go. Puddles are there to be splashed in, trees to be climbed, insects to be examined, and hills to be rolled down.

Walks are adventures to children, who allow their imaginations to lead them. An adult walking through a field may see only grass and hedges, but a child taking the same walk may be going on their own bear hunt. Children are not afraid to lie down in the grass as part of their game, to get dirty, and be a part of the nature around them. Walking at this stage is great fun.

Lots of young children read the magical story of *Jack and the Beanstalk* and then take a seed home to plant and grow. Nature needs food, water, and light—the same elements as we do—for its survival. The story of Jack climbing to the top of that huge beanstalk may inspire children to head out and climb their own hills and mountains. From an early age, while waiting for their bean to grow, a child is learning to adopt the pace of nature.

LEARNING LESSONS OUTDOORS

As children progress at school and spend more time inside, the connection with nature can start to fade. Increasing screen time and the popularity of social media are leading to a different way of playing and learning. Some countries adopt outdoor learning, and the growing popularity of forest schools and outdoor clubs reveals our need to spend more time walking in nature, and less time sitting.

> "THERE ARE GOOD THINGS
> AROUND US EVERY SINGLE DAY
> AND WE DON'T NEED TO TRAVEL
> TO EXPERIENCE THEM"

My three children attend the "Outdoors Project" after school and during vacations. They learn a whole range of skills, from communication and social skills to hand–eye coordination, building, and engineering. The project teaches all curriculum-based subjects, such as Stone Age to Iron Age, Celts to Romans, survival, foraging, muddy math, and geography. The learning opportunities are endless and often much more engaging for those who struggle with a formal classroom setting. The children come home tired, happy, and full of stories about their adventures.

GEESE FLYING UP HIGH

When we become adults, our lives get so busy and relentless, and we often head from A to B without looking around us. We hear geese flying overhead but fail to stop and consider why they are all calling to one another and how they know to move at a particular time of day to a new place. Where are they headed? They are moving for their survival.

I have traveled and I have stayed put, and I continue to work through the journey of grief, with the loss of my father now—a new journey in itself. What have I learned?

Nature and human life closely parallel each other. Nothing lasts forever; it will all pass. What goes around eventually comes around. After spring comes summer, then fall and winter in an unchanging cycle.

Sorrow and regret should not drag us down. There are good things around us every single day and we don't need to travel to experience them. The flowers sprouting through the cracks in the sidewalk signal that winter is coming to an end. Early-morning waking to birdsong can lift us out of our beds to investigate what the new day will bring. A simple walk can clear our heads, give us a fresh outlook on the day, and inevitably make us feel better at the same time. We can take pleasure in growing some flowers from bulb to vase, enjoying the simple routine of watering and feeding them. Life can knock us down, but we manage to get up, whether we realize it or not.

GET THE NATURE HABIT

Ideas for accessing ancient wisdom

1 | LUNCH AL FRESCO

Could you have lunch in a green space outside at least once a week? Find a place you love. When you return, what changes can you notice since your last visit?

2 | NATURE INSIDE

Could you bring a plant or fresh flowers into your home or office? Notice the little lift it brings. Observe how easily a moment spent providing food, water, and nurture slips into the daily routine.

3 | TINY FARM

Where in your living space could you grow some herbs or salad leaves, or sprout some beans? Rosemary can boost concentration, and mint lends calmness. Sense the joy in consuming your creation.

4 | FLUFFY CLOUDS

When stress creeps in, look up at the clouds. Just like your thoughts, clouds come and go. Couple a worry with a cloud and watch it disappear across the sky.

5 | LOVELY SCRUFFS

Can you notice how, in any natural space, there is chaos within the calm? Twigs and leaves strewn across the grass, patches of mud—nothing is neat and tidy and yet everything functions well.

6 | HILL WALKING

Can you choose a hill to walk up? Be aware of the determination in yourself to keep climbing. The next time you come across a problem, try to remind yourself of the sensation and feel your strength.

ONE

FOOT

IN

FRONT

OF
THE
OTHER

ONE FOOT IN
FRONT OF THE OTHER

Walking through a challenge

Gert-Jan de Hoon | Voyage Beyond

A group of visually impaired walkers, accompanied by their personal buddies, arrived at Praza Obradoiro in Santiago de Compostela, Spain, in October 2015. After 14 days spent walking together, everyone realized that life would be different forever.

The group completed a pilgrimage of 124 miles. The limitations on their sight meant they had to let go of the idea of having control over their life during the expedition. Getting through the journey meant trusting a buddy to walk with and accepting help to find their way around. The buddy was there for everything from navigating the *albergues* (pilgrims' hostels) to ordering meals, and finding the washrooms. This is the story of what the walk brought to the people with a visual impairment, but it is equally the story of the buddies who traveled beside them and the insights the experience gave them.

THE CAMINO DE SANTIAGO

According to legend, the tomb of St. James, who had been a disciple of Jesus, was found in about 814. He had been beheaded in Jerusalem by King Herod Agrippa I in the year 44 C.E., during the persecutions of Christians. His body had been taken to Galicia in Spain and buried at the place now called Santiago de Compostela. Eight centuries later, his grave was found as the result of a hermit, Pelayo, having a vision of a bright, shining star, surrounded by a circle

" "

AFTER
14 DAYS
SPENT
WALKING
TOGETHER,
EVERYONE
REALIZED
THAT LIFE
WOULD BE
DIFFERENT
FOREVER

of smaller stars, pointing to the burial site. After learning about the discovery and rumors of miracles in the area, King Alfonso II journeyed from Oviedo to the site to venerate the relics, proclaiming St. James the patron saint of Spain, and he ordered the building of a church and shrine to St. James. His journey is considered to be the first pilgrimage to Santiago.

For over a thousand years Santiago de Compostela has been an important place of worship in Europe. The Camino de Santiago (pilgrimage route to Santiago) has been highly traveled, with more than half a million people a year embarking on the journey in the 13th century. In those days, pilgrimages had a religious basis, and pilgrims traveled to the tomb of St. James to worship the relics and for penance. By the early 1980s there were only a handful of pilgrims walking the Camino, but since then there has been a huge increase in people making the journey.

People walk the Camino for different reasons today. Some go because of the cultural heritage, others see it as a physical challenge, and many walk for a more spiritual reason. They step out of their busy and demanding lives for a short period to walk and reflect. The Christian ideology would explain the pilgrimage as a time to witness the beauty of nature that God has created. Whether you hold beliefs about God or not, there is a connection with the spiritual that happens for many when exploring the natural environment and meeting other people on a similar journey.

People come to Spain from all over the world to walk this famous pilgrimage route. According to the Confraternity of Saint James, 277,915 pilgrims arrived in Santiago in 2016, receiving a *Compostela*, a certificate written in Latin confirming their completion of the pilgrimage.

My work is as a coach and guide who, in many different ways, walks beside people on their journey. I aim to listen and observe without judgment and offer what feels right when a traveler's feet falter. When I first began doing it, the idea of being a part of this venture filled me with inspiration. I wondered how it would take shape and what I might learn on the way.

DREAMING WITHOUT SIGHT

Imagine that you are blind or visually impaired, and you would like to walk the Camino de Santiago. What do you do? Annemieke Oost, who had been visually impaired for eight years, asked me this question because I had walked to Santiago several times, in different seasons. She was dreaming of walking the Camino and wondered whether I felt it would be possible for her to achieve this dream. Knowing what it is to live with sight can make it harder when it is lost. There are changes to the familiar to adapt to, and a whole new way of navigating the world to learn. Annemieke's dream showed bravery but also showed what she had managed in adapting to her new world over the previous decade. I found it both moving and inspiring that she had reached a point where she was ready to dream of taking on a challenge that would make even many people with full sight apprehensive.

While going for a walk together and pondering the question of how she could walk the Camino, we wondered whether there were other people with a visual or visual/auditory disability who also had the same kind of dream but imagined that they would never be able to do it. This first question led to more:

- What would be possible (and not possible) on a pilgrimage for someone with a visual or visual/auditory impairment?

- What would be needed to organize a pilgrimage for a group of people with these needs?

- How would a pilgrim with a visual or visual/auditory disability experience walking the Camino?

- How could we capture and share this experience to create greater understanding and insight and inspire others?

- How could we best support and challenge people to step out of their comfort zone and explore the unknown?

As a result, we decided to initiate Camino Walking Blind, to assist young people with a visual or visual/auditory disability to make this walk.

" "

IT WAS A
COMPLETE
SPECTRUM
OF EMOTIONS
AND THAT
IS WHAT
I LOVED

BEING A BUDDY

For the pilgrimage from Ponferrada to Santiago de Compostela, we selected five walkers and five buddies. Every walker with a visual or visual/auditory disability would be guided by a personal buddy who would share their eyes.

The plan was to walk 124 miles in 14 days, with an average distance of about 9 miles per day. Carrying our own backpacks, we would stay in *albergues* on the way and eat in the villages we were going to pass through or where we would stay for the night. Luggage would be transported by our own bus, which would double as a backup or emergency vehicle if required.

We had no budget, we were not sure what was possible or how far we would be able to walk, and we had no idea how intense it would be for the buddies to be assisting 24/7 for 14 days. What thoughts, emotions, and challenges would surface during the pilgrimage?

Walkers and buddies applied to take part by writing a letter about what motivated them to join the journey. We were looking for enthusiasm and a willingness to learn. In June, three months after our initial decision, we invited a selected group for an interview, and by the end of the month we had our team.

We had made a first big step. By this time, we realized that the project was getting serious. Articles appeared in regional newspapers and magazines, and we were invited to speak on the radio about Camino Walking Blind. The finances began falling into place and we could give the project the go-ahead.

A team-building weekend was organized for the end of August. This would be the first time we had spent a few days together as a group. It was a time to walk together and get to know one another better.

Buddies were getting prepared and experiencing walking blindfolded. They learned what it felt like to follow and trust the person guiding them. We practiced different ways of nonverbal communication and spoke about safety. The weekend was a priceless experience.

WALKERS' EXPERIENCES

Marjolein

"Thanks to the buddies, I could make this journey. They explained where we were walking, about the vegetation, and how the houses and churches looked. I have tasted the atmosphere, felt the earth, smelled the flavors, and enjoyed the Spanish food and wonderful wines. I was connected with my buddy by holding a light metal frame, which gave me the feeling of walking independently while being guided away from obstacles on the way. This way it was possible to talk and experience it all in a very relaxed way. Walking the Camino, I have experienced a feeling of being completely free."

Maartje

"My mental space was completely filled with finding a new way to deal with being deaf and blind (Usher syndrome) in the extreme situation of being simultaneously in an unknown country, spending every night at a different hostel, walking unknown routes, being guided every day by someone I barely knew, and carrying a backpack. As I learned new routines I began to relax. Every day I felt more grounded; gradually I could let go of the heaviness of my Usher syndrome. I discovered calm in the simplicity of the Camino: eating, walking, reflecting. This routine allowed me to be more in my physical body and less in survival mode, filled with the mental processes in my head. It gave me space to think."

Connie

"I have been confronted with myself a few times. The moment you realize that you can't make a walk like this on your own, and you have no control over it, hurts inside. It is those little things you experience, such as how slowly you pack your bag, because you are looking for things and can't see to find them."

Willemijn

"My convulsive need of 'wanting and having to do everything myself' is gone—I am more at ease with my disability. I have experienced how nice it is to let people 'help' you (next to devices and a guide dog at home). The complexity involved in 'accepting help to keep direction in my life' was just a concept in my mind. To walk so easily, only being connected to your buddy with two fingers, has been one of the most powerful experiences of the Camino!"

" "

I CAN LOOK
AT MYSELF
AND OTHERS
AGAIN WITH A
SMILE. I FEEL
SATISFIED
WITH MY LIFE
EXPERIENCES.

Séverine

Séverine

"My experience of walking the Way and being part of the Camino Walking Blind team was very intense. My intensity was felt as sadness and confrontation, but also as happiness, beauty, and joy. It was a complete spectrum of emotions and that is what I loved. I had to let go of certain ideas on the Camino and I realize now, after returning home, that I want to hold onto this new insight. What a contradiction!

"How I miss the views. How I do miss the hugs, though at the same time I am aware that this Camino cocoon is just a partial reality. The challenge is to put into practice in my ordinary life what I have 'learned.' In Spain, I didn't need energy management; despite the short nights I had lots of energy. I must look after my energy again, back in Holland. Am I stepping back into old patterns? I don't think so.

"Walking the Camino, I have learned that I do like a challenge, and that I don't even mind not being able to go on expeditions on my own any more. Actually, it is more fun with two or in a group. My renewed self-confidence makes Usher syndrome less present. I can look at myself and others again with a smile. I feel satisfied with my life experiences. My fears about the future are still there—not being able to see someone's smile any more is a horrifying thought that I cannot and will not think about. Anyhow, I am feeling more connected again with myself and others."

BUDDIES' EXPERIENCES

Anja

"Life simplifies to core values: intense meetings, walking to your next destination, eating, drinking, and sleeping in a bed. This journey has given me more insight about the important things in life, about what makes me happy. I have fewer doubts about myself—I feel stronger in who I am. Most valuable was the solidarity: how we did this together and had faith in each other. The words of Marjolein, on the last evening at Monte de Gozo, touched me deeply: 'You can experience beauty without seeing. I know this and I have experienced it again.'"

Henk

"We have been singing, dancing, crying, eating, and drinking together: team-building in its optimum form. A day less walking than we have planned? We adjust, because we are a team. A day traveling by taxi with a walker who didn't feel fit was one of my best days. I also have learned that you don't always have to do something; you can let go of being over-responsible. After this journey, I have even more respect for people with a visual disability."

Jantina

"This journey was my first time traveling with a group of people I hardly knew. It was so special to experience becoming a very close group in such a short time. Walking the Camino I have learned that it is about who you are and not about what you do. Mutual differences (partly) disappear.

"Most important for myself was the experience of finding a balance between giving and receiving. I can do both and, in doing so, I have learned that by opening myself up to receive, I can show a bit more of myself and am able to let others get closer.

65

"Back home, I mostly miss living in the moment, the simplicity of life on the Camino, the ease in connecting, even with strangers, and the slowness that automatically happens when you are walking."

THE JOURNEY CONTINUES

We went back the following year with a new group of walkers and buddies. Again, it was a big success and we had a new experience of walking the Camino. A film crew followed us during our journey this time to make a documentary.

Now we are preparing for another journey, and what we have learned from walkers and buddies alike will continue to shape our next steps with the project.

We want to slowly grow a movement that gets people in motion by connecting and undertaking walks together.

THE CAMINO HAS STAYED WITH US

Every member of our group witnessed what it meant to walk together with a sense of equality and mutual respect. The motion and rhythm of walking carried us through—it continued regardless of rain, sunshine, or wind. Every day was a new story of giving and receiving. A sort of blind faith and willingness to step outside our comfort zone grew throughout the walk. We found a rhythm to match the movement of our soles in the process of giving and receiving. This has remained with us all and has left within us a desire to share this with others we encounter daily.

The happiness and sense of completeness you feel when supporting another person through a challenge such as this are enough to lift you out of any low mood or inward-focused worrying. When you are someone else's eyes, you need to pay attention and not drift off into your own thoughts. This demands a presence and a sensitivity that banish any space in the mind for anxiety or self-doubt. The sensation is liberating and enhances the connection with your partner. Together you are focused only on the next step. Yet the world seems huge, complex, and beautiful while not being something to worry about. On the intersection of giving and receiving we became closer and ever more understanding of each other.

We gained so much from the mental and physical challenge of carrying our own things, being self-sufficient, and feeling the strength and potential of our bodies. When you push through one physical boundary, you can't help but imagine what the next one might be that you can find and overcome. Push by push, step by step, it becomes no distance at all.

The pace is so slow and rhythmic. There is time to bathe in all the senses and savor each sensation. When you are beside people whose senses work in a different way, you notice how one sense has strengthened when the other has faded. If they can do this, then can't we all develop the capacity to become more attuned to our world, one sense at a time?

As with many big events and adventures in life, our final and most valuable learning is finding how we can do the same big stuff in small ways every day.

GET THE WALKING BUDDY HABIT

Ideas for getting communities outside

1 | WHO?

Who might hesitate in talking their first steps outside in your local community? Maybe this is you, or maybe it is an elderly neighbor? Maybe an anxious friend? Where might your buddy be hiding?

2 | THE PROPOSITION

The internet can be a great way to find others looking for someone to walk with. Could you suggest a first small local outing? Mention the benefits to you first—everyone loves to help others.

3 | THE FIRST WALK

The first walk is a time to bond and agree how you will stroll together. Gently ask questions and listen to their story. Find an opportunity to begin to share what brought you both to this point.

4 | THE HABIT

Having a regular slot makes it easier to form a habit. Plan a routine together. A buddy can be an inspiration to get outside and also a nudge to push yourself rather than let someone down.

5 | REFLECTING

Habits stick when we reflect on what we have achieved through the steps we've made. Weave into your conversation moments when you share this together. Make it conscious and regular.

6 | SPREADING

How could you share your buddy story with others? Who else do you both know whom you could "match-make" as walking buddies? Who else in your community might like to get involved?

CHAPTER 5

WALKING

CITY WALKING

Calm in the chaos

Clare Barry | Urban Curiosity

Did you know that *inspirare* means "to inhale" in Latin? Think about it. City life is frenetic. We rush through our days reviewing mental to-do lists, ruminating about past conversations, fretting over future plans. We spend more time online than we do sleeping. We feel there is never enough time to think, play, or create, and we struggle with digital overwhelm. It is no wonder that so many of us feel frazzled and creatively unfulfilled. It turns out that inspiration doesn't strike when we race from here to there without a moment to catch our breath.

70

The problem is that it can cost us our physical and mental wellbeing, our relationships, and our happiness. How can we thrive here and not be consumed by the city's relentless chaos?

POWERFUL FOOTSTEPS

A simple walk can help. The city can be a multisensory smorgasbord, and many of us passively consume messages and stimuli all day long while our mind whirls with regrets or worries. A stroll where we notice what is out there and the emotions it provokes in us is the first step in becoming less stressed.

Planting our feet on the ground feels definitive when life is a series of unknowns. Air hitting our cheeks wakes us up or soothes us. Our heartbeat quickens and our hamstrings stretch with each stride. We detect shisha smoke outside a café or pass by an extractor fan and get a whiff of fried foods, triggering reminiscences of high school.

" "

WHEN WE ARE
INTENTIONAL
ABOUT USING
THIS MOBILE
TECHNOLOGY,
WE RECLAIM
CONTROL

We wait for the traffic lights to change and we gulp exhaust-flavored air. There are other aromas lingering on our tongue: morning coffee and jam. We lick our lips and get a hit of berry or mint (lip gloss perhaps, or maybe a dab of leftover toothpaste in the corner of our mouth?).

Vehicles trundle past and we notice all the colors, textures, and angles of our street: the humans, animals, movement, stillness. Perhaps we see our initials on a billboard or find the rude word written on that dirty truck window amusing.

We run the flat of our hand over brick walls, smooth metal rails, and glass doors. We touch our fingertips to a flyer wrapped around a lamppost. We zone out car horns and sirens, bus engines, and bicycle brakes. We hear shrieks of laughter from teenage school students and make a rapid assessment of them based on their wardrobe and their slang and syntax. On a construction site, sheet metal is dragged over scaffolding—it sounds like thunder and we look skyward to interpret the clouds.

"PLANTING OUR FEET ON THE
GROUND FEELS DEFINITIVE WHEN
LIFE IS A SERIES OF UNKNOWNS"

We walk on and become curious about what prompted that taxi driver's gesture and the woman's scowl as she leaves the Post Office. We wonder about how the graffiti artist managed to reach the advertising billboard and realize the paving slabs underfoot have the texture of the sun-worshipper's décolletage. We dare to make eye contact with fellow citizens and are rewarded occasionally. We spot the shrub in the little gated square and think about the passage of time as we study its branches, which may be budding or discarding leaves.

CHOOSING TO DAWDLE

Saunter, stroll, meander, or mooch—a casual pace works best. I like to stroll but prefer to dawdle. This verb means to waste time, to idle; it also signifies moving slowly or languidly. I used to think dawdling was for toddlers and tourists. Like millions of other Londoners—and urbanites the world over—I walked, talked, and texted simultaneously. I dated, socialized, and networked via touchscreen technology. I tracked my calories, steps, and sleep quality. I went to bed with my smartphone under my pillow, replied to my boss/clients/colleagues before bedtime, and suffered from insomnia.

I averted my gaze on public transit and wore my busy status as a badge of honor. I stashed high heels underneath my desk and switched to sneakers for my commute. Dawdling was for other people. Worst of all, I'd left my creativity at the bottom of the career ladder sometime around the beginning of the new millennium. I seldom indulged in daydreaming or allowed my environment to inspire me.

SWITCHED ON BUT DISCONNECTED
For five years I ignored the message my body tried to deliver. I would not yield to this inconvenient development or adjust my lifestyle beyond the bare minimum required in the most acute moments of agony. In time my dreams were filled with escapes to mountaintop cabins and vows of silence. Walking, working, sitting, and sleeping became impossible, and surgery inevitable.

My life changed when I had an operation on my lumbar spine. No more would I complain about never having enough time, while frittering away hours online. Turns out I didn't have to leave the Big City and pursue silence on top of a mountain. In fact, I fell back in love with London's sparkling lights once I discovered how to avoid being dazzled by them.

DISPOSABLE PANTIES AND SURGICAL STOCKINGS
There is nothing quite like these to make a gal feel foxy, especially when she can't put them on unassisted. It was a hazy spring morning and the nurse at the hospital helped me with my fancy new fashion accessories. While I waited to be taken to the operating theater, I gazed out the window at the cityscape, never having imagined how important walking along its streets would be to my physical recovery and creative reconnection.

" "

I INVITE YOU
TO REMEMBER
THE POWER AND
SIMPLICITY OF
DAWDLING, IDLING
WHEREVER YOU
ARE RIGHT NOW

Twenty-four hours later, my rock-star neurologist sent me home with nothing more than minimal pain relief and instructions to take a daily walk. The first outing around my neighborhood was tentative. I had nowhere to be and nothing to do except move one foot in front of the other.

SOMETHING UNEXPECTED HAPPENED

My body hurt with each footstep and yet this slower pace allowed urban vignettes to unfold before me: a quirky shop window, the whiff of fresh gloss paint, an exchange of smiles, childish chatter from a local playground, the warmth of spring sunshine on my cheeks, a magnolia tree in full bloom, the distant rumble of a subway train.

In the same month, researchers at Stanford University reported that walking boosted creativity by up to 60 percent. I didn't know this as I moved along the street like a robot. This simple rhythmic movement that I had done without thinking—until I couldn't—sparked a million questions in me while my anxious thoughts melted away. I felt an urgency to spill words across a blank page. Despite this, my return home did not involve velocity; instead I ambled back, filled with creative possibility and joy.

These short everyday strolls changed my life. The lens through which I viewed my native city had changed and it was exhilarating.

INSPIRATION WAS EVERYWHERE WHEN I STOPPED LONG ENOUGH TO BREATHE

Less rushing around town and hurrying into the future helped me take in what had always been there. My convalescent strolls were along ordinary residential streets, but I found delight and inspiration all around. I believe the act of moving our bodies changes gears in our brains, making space for connections and reflections. The Stanford study found that walking boosted a person's creative output regardless of whether they were outside in the fresh air or inside on a treadmill in a windowless basement gym facing a blank wall. Whether it is washing our hair or walking, the scene is different from the moment before, and our motion is repetitive and rhythmic, requiring only mild exertion; our attention is unfocused and we zone out from quotidian worries and desires, then our mind drifts off again. In this way, insights and ideas emerge. It is the same reason why so many of us have "lightbulb moments" in the shower.

GET INTO THE SLOW LANE

Dawdling gave me the courage to choose the slow lane in a city addicted to speed, to cultivate my curiosity and, later, to embark on a new way of working. How could any of that be labeled a waste of time?

There's one problem with this mode of transportation: it is not conducive to urban life. And yet it might just be the key to thriving here. Most of the world is hyperconnected, and the World Health Organization estimates that 70 percent of us will be urban dwellers within the next 30 or so years. The calmer and more connected to ourselves and our communities we can be, the better that time will look.

I believe we need to focus on how we spend our time, energy, and attention. Consider these verbs: we "pay" attention, we "spend" time and energy, we never "have" enough time. We often tend to fritter away these scarce and finite resources.

That keyhole surgery was indeed transformative in every area of my life, and those slow walks helped me disconnect to reconnect. Soon after, I ambled out of my dream job as cofounder of the London School of Economics and Political Science's entrepreneurship hub and became a flâneuse, author, and business owner.

ON SEEING THINGS DIFFERENTLY

My work today combines all my favorite post-burnout discoveries: slow walking, exploring the urban environment while noticing, questioning, and sparking ideas, then writing about them. I help stressed-out urbanites get more creative and consider their relationship with their digital lives, and to reclaim time and headspace for what matters to them in real life.

By observing what we pay attention to during each block of 24 hours, we often realize how we spend it on things that, in the end, are not important to us. We don't need to wait until summer vacation or, worse, retirement to pursue our dreams now.

An Urban Curiosity Walkshop is a two-hour creativity session and digital detox—on foot. I lead them in person in London and offer resources for individuals to download and print off. At the beginning of each session, I give participants a small notebook and pencil, then invite them to switch their cellphones off or to silent mode so they can give their full attention to discovering what emerges during the walkshop. When marketing the walkshops originally, I found that "digital detox" resonated more with people than "digital mindfulness." At this point in the session, I explain that I prefer the latter because the former suggests the technology is toxic when, in fact, it is how we engage with it that can be detrimental to us. When we are intentional about using this mobile technology, we reclaim control and use it as it was designed to be used: to enhance the way we live and work.

"WE ARE TOO BUSY TO OPEN UP TO POSSIBILITY OR FEEL THE JOY OF HUMAN CONNECTION IN OUR COMMUNITIES"

I created each walkshop route to help busy people slow down and see things differently. We urbanites are so busy and hyperconnected that we are missing out on small moments of beauty and wonder in our neighborhoods. We are too busy to open up to possibility or feel the joy of human connection in our communities. These are the things that make us feel alive and calm, inspired and happy.

For tips on how to do a walkshop in your own neighborhood, see the end of this chapter.

CITY WALKING IS THE KEY TO CALM

It is a thrill to witness walkshop participants having revelations about the power of walking as a tool for mindfulness and thriving in the city. A graphic designer said she created stuff every day but it was on-demand and according to the client's requirements. Her epiphany was discovering the need to write poetry again—inspired by her surroundings—simply for the sake of being creative.

A mother felt sick at the prospect of a decade of monotony spent driving the kids to school up to four times a day in term-time. After her walkshop, she viewed this journey as an opportunity to engage with her children and notice the minutiae of the street. A leaf might be on the pavement on the way to school, and on her return she might spot it in the gutter. Simple but helpful in reducing all her usual frantic thoughts.

Once, a computer whizz kid confessed that the farthest he ever walked was from home to car and car to office. He had forgotten what it felt like to mooch and meander, and saw how unfamiliar he was with the local community; he realized he wanted to discover more.

SAY GOODBYE TO CHAOS AND HELLO TO DELIGHT

We don't have to exit our lives stage left to thrive and delight in the city. Back during my high-flying career-gal days, I could have made different choices and taken small steps—literal and figurative—and thus avoided total burnout. I don't regret the lessons I gained from that time, and I invite you to remember the power and simplicity of dawdling, idling wherever you are right now.

Wander, wonder, and make space for calm, connection, and discovery. Meaningful revelations await. Are you ready?

HOW TO DO A WALKSHOP

Ideas for discovering calm in the chaos

1 | CLAW BACK

Whether or not you take lunch breaks, or you have twin toddlers and leaving the house is hard, claw back time from your jam-packed schedule, even if you work on an unattractive industrialized area or it's raining outside.

2 | FIRE UP…

…your senses. Assess how you are feeling in your head and locate where your body is holding that sensation. Take that first step and notice your heel striking the ground, the arch of your foot curving, and each of your toes making contact with the floor. How do they feel in your shoes?

3 | INHALE

Feel your lungs inflate and your shoulders drop as you breathe out. What smells are in your environment? What do you hear? How does the air feel on your skin? Swallow and take notice of what flavors and tastes linger on your tongue.

4 | TUNE IN

Search for the color red in the cityscape. Shades and tones of it will present themselves everywhere: on corporate logos, lips, cars, clothing, graffiti. Next, pick a letter of the alphabet and search for it in the street: on architecture, window frames, iron railings, garden squares. Hunt for the letters of your name or quirky words in shop frontages. Look for shapes and lines; think about textures and materials.

5 | PAUSE

If you brought pen and paper with you, free-write for one minute about what you recall about your journey from your starting point to this point. Write down words or sentences, or make doodles.

accessories, behavior, and general vibe. Make eye contact with this person or someone else. Smile.

6 | PERSPECTIVE

Change your point of view: pause and crouch down to look up at a ghost sign. Cross over the road and spot differences you'd never notice on your habitual route.

7 | GET MOVING

Study the buildings or houses on the street. Look for old jammed next to new; notice red bricks next to shiny glass and metal. Search for the joins and symmetry; imagine what the walls would say if they could speak.

8 | OBSERVE

Who is around you? Pick a person and give them a name. Where are they from and what is their destination? What drew you to this individual? How would you describe them to the police in the event of an incident? Observe their clothing, footwear, facial expression,

DAWDLE AND

DAWDLE AND DOODLE

Journaling the journey

Antonia Thompson | Artist at Phoenix Brighton and
former Editor at *The Huffington Post*, AOL, Sky, and ITV

I feel completely ridiculous. Rain is hammering down so hard on the hood of
my bright blue waterproof jacket that my hair is already soaked. Apparently,
I think it's still completely fine to continue my walk along the seafront, even
if I have to keep stopping to cling to a lamppost.

The sea is howling at me like a hyena, its ever-changing slabs of wave
resembling the inside of a washing machine. I should have taken my own advice
and got a dog, though I wouldn't subject a pet to this.

"What are you doing? Haven't you read those news stories about people
getting blown into moving traffic?" I hear the inner chatter start like the choke
on a rickety old car. I laugh out loud at it. No one has heard, thank goodness—
there are few people insane enough to approach this unwelcoming promenade
today. My only company is some windswept scaffolders who are looking none
too pleased at the prospect of assembling poles on the façade of an ice-cream
store. The seagulls haven't even bothered to get up.

I start running to battle the wind. "Running? You hate running," says the inner
voice. It's funny what benefits come out of a regular walk—like fitness. I've
been taking daily walks for a while now and I've got faster at working through
the resistance provided by my mind-chatter. In fact, I'm starting to enjoy
combating it as part of the process.

" "

WRITING
FREED
ME
FROM
MENIAL
TASKS

I'm genuinely excited about the remarkable change in the sea from yesterday. That's why I come here; the waves bring new reams of emotion with every changing tide. I get my phone out and take photographs, taking about 15 very quickly, and try to scribble a line or two in my sketchbook before skedaddling.

It's a surprise how far out the tide is. I can even see exposed sand beyond the pebbles. I love that sand. When I first moved to Brighton, on Britain's south coast, I couldn't take my four-month-old daughter on the beach because she would try to eat those pebbles. Every year now, we seem to be getting more sand. Maybe. Or I just never noticed it before these walks. I laugh into the salty wind as I think of the absurdity of my situation and wonder how I got here.

A CREATIVE JOURNEY

Somewhere lurking in the bottom of a drawer in your home is there an unused sketchpad? Perhaps hidden from sight are some unopened oil-paints, grown-up modeling clay, or a beautiful, untouched notebook with a moleskin cover. Of course it was you who bought that very expensive digital SLR camera and never even took it on vacation in case it got broken.

The intention was always there for creativity, I'm certain. But, deep down, you're scared. Well, I am anyway, constantly. The very thought of reaching beyond a carefully constructed comfort zone can be terrifying. And when it comes to creativity, inner chatter can really put a downer on things. "I don't know how, I haven't got time, it won't pay the bills, who do I think I am? I've got nothing to say, it's too late…" I could go on.

I can find all sorts of reasons not to create.

I have a vivid memory of my ten-year-old self attempting to draw a cartoon strip about gnomes. I should have known better, but I showed it to my older sister's friend who was a "natural" at caricatures and she burst out laughing. The next time she came to our house she had sketched a brilliant cartoon, inspired by my "bad" drawing, with me as chief gnome. It was entitled "Tiddles: Why I Didn't Draw the Pictures".

So what I "learned" from this experience is that I shouldn't even bother trying because it would make me empty and sad. And what *you* have probably learned is that I shared a childhood nickname with a fair few cats.

What I should have told myself was, "Never mind, at least you gave it a go, and practice makes perfect. If that doesn't work out, then maybe you could try to convey the same thing through collage or photography. And if you really want to be a cartoonist, they're going to invent computers that can do this sort of thing in the future, so it will make it much easier to learn."

"THE VERY THOUGHT OF
REACHING BEYOND A CAREFULLY
CONSTRUCTED COMFORT ZONE
CAN BE TERRIFYING"

I did actually make it to art college because, despite that setback, lots of people admired my creative spirit as a child, and in the end those voices won. I fell in love with creativity on my Art Foundation course and then studied Fine Art in Scotland. I graduated in the early 1990s, which was a time when you were encouraged to go on welfare after college and carry on making art. Instead, faced with a life of being really pretentious while living in a tiny apartment, I found office jobs and eventually retrained in media.

Writing freed me from menial tasks, office politics involving catfights over who got to hold the camera, and listening to presentations. I loved it for a while, but soon found out that writers don't get paid a living wage and managers do. Any honest office worker will tell you that moving up the career ladder involves sacrificing the very thing that lured you into that career in the first place. I remember talking to a civil servant on a commuter train, and during our journey we worked out that we pretty much had the same job.

I moved from London to Brighton for maternity leave, for which I will be eternally grateful to my old company—they gave me a whole year with my newborn baby. Returning to work was a different story. I endured the daily

" "

THE PATH
TO CREATIVE
FREEDOM
IS RIDDLED WITH
SELF-DOUBT.
THE BEST WAY TO
FREE YOURSELF
FROM THE FEAR
IS TO WALK.

four-hour commute for three years until I reached burnout, by which point the flame of creativity was dulled almost to extinction. I decided to go back to the start and make art.

The path to creative freedom is riddled with self-doubt. The best way to free yourself from the fear is to walk.

FIRST STEPS BACK TO IMAGINATIVE THINKING

I remember the first walk for the silence and space it gave me. It was a walk with my partner to the seafront. He had to force me to go in the direction opposite to that of the train station. I was at my most frazzled and anxious and had just decided I wasn't going back to work. We simply talked—it was calm, sweet. The nicest thing was acknowledging that my legs were free to move where they wanted, not to the train station and not up busy London streets while trying not to bump into other commuters.

Now I walk all the time. This year, as the result of an accidental New Year's Resolution, I downloaded a 10,000-steps-a-day walking app, and now I simply have to do it.

I've brought the walks into my artwork, and the things I see on my journey often inspire me. At the moment I photograph and paint the waves on the seafront. As a result I've almost completely extinguished my fear of the blank page. For me, walking is like activating the canvas, starting the creative process by making space in my mind. I treat walking as my journaling time, when I touch base with my inner artist. On a walk I take photographs, write things down, or sketch to exorcise any inner ramblings. The more I walk, the more I look, the more I listen, the more I am inspired by all my senses. Art isn't just about the visual.

In her book *A Mindfulness Guide for the Frazzled*, Ruby Wax talks about how your brain can't prioritize senses and thoughts at the same time. If you concentrate on immersing yourself in your environment via your senses— hearing the crunch of pebbles underfoot or a seagull squawking—then your inner dialogue will fade into the background.

The key thing I remind myself of when walking is that there's no pressure to get to the point of inspiration where everything is flowing and I am in the zone. There are scientific reasons why creativity can have trouble flourishing under stressful conditions.

You know that feeling when you can't think straight and you can't find what a yogi calls your "center"? That could be due to your body overproducing the hormone cortisol, which can wreak havoc. It starts making lots of neural connections in the part of your brain that is responsible for fear, and those connections in turn make more connections, creating a vicious circle of stress. (For more about cortisol and the part it plays, see Chapter 9, page 130.)

LEARNING FROM OTHER ARTISTS

For some artists the process becomes the work, be it walking, journaling, sketching, or even dancing. The key thing to remember when kickstarting your creative process is that it involves your thoughts, feelings, emotions, senses, mission, desires, scribbles—nobody else's—and you don't have to show *your* creations to anyone if you don't want to. But some do, and are revered for doing so.

Making giant sketchbooks

"Turn Back Now", an exhibition by Keith Tyson at the Jerwood Gallery, in Hastings, in southeastern England, in 2017, showed a series of studio wall drawings representing 20 years of Tyson's life in the form of giant diary entries. Hung frame to frame across five rooms, the 360 works comprised pictures and words in an eclectic mix of mediums and styles. Each drawing represented a creative pause, a moment or event, good or bad, that had inspired him in life.

Sculpting from nature

Andy Goldsworthy is a sculptor who works with materials only available in nature. In his book *Time*, he explores the changing of the seasons and the anticipation of each one. An example of his work is *Cairn* from 1999, a conelike stone structure that he built on a sandy beach in between the tides. The work was washed away by the sea eventually and all that remained were his photographs of the process, his visual journal.

When walking is art
Turner Prize-winning artist Richard Long goes for a walk and describes it as art. The resulting gallery exhibitions might show a stunning black-and-white photo, an arrangement of slate stones in a giant X-shape, or a textural painting of a field encompassing a whole wall. But whatever his choice of visual representation, there is always a simple, poetic description of the walk beside it, in a beautiful typeface; image and text sit together harmoniously.

Long's walks can take him hours or even weeks. They may involve traveling through urban environments, though he chooses not to document those parts, preferring more isolated, often wild, empty spaces.

Ideas really can come from nowhere—you just have to go looking for them.

Other creatives' ways of walking
Novelist Naomi Alderman uses walking in a highly productive and creative way, choosing to alternate writing with walking for 15-minute periods.

Comedian Demetri Martin finds walking essential for writing jokes, and when he can't face the rain he walks at his treadmill desk, allowing his brain to stay active and productive at the same time.

Comedy is also a great way to relax your neural pathways and let in the creativity. The psychiatrist William Fry studied this for 30 years and found that laughter can lower your cortisol levels.

BREAKING THROUGH CREATIVE RESISTANCE
Many great artists and poets have used walking and journaling as a tool for creativity, and so can you. These people didn't start out as fully formed artists; finding inspiration is like a muscle that you have to exercise.

No matter how latent your talent, your brain still has the capacity to adapt and change. Neuroplasticity is a scientific term that denotes the brain's ability to rewire and resculpt itself. So even if you feel you are a little set in your ways, if you want to change, it is possible. New situations and activities can help your nerve cells to adjust and create a whole new way of thinking. You don't have to hold on to childhood fears or lifelong beliefs about what you *are* or what you think you *should* be doing—you're in the driving seat. And if you want to start your creative journey, there's no time like the present.

Use your stream of consciousness

From the premise that everyone is creative, author Julia Cameron suggests in *The Artist's Way* that you write "morning pages," which can unlock your creativity. She suggests that as soon as you wake up, before you do anything else, you write three pages of whatever is on your mind. Don't read through them or show them to anyone. This has the effect of getting rid of unwanted emotions, stops the inner critic from kicking in, and makes way for all the good creativity to come out afterward.

Journaling has the added benefit of being good for your health. Dr. James W Pennebaker, author of *Writing to Heal*, has studied people who write a journal and has observed that they visit the doctor less than they did before writing. The benefit doesn't depend on whether the writing gets read or not.

Walk through it

Scientists at Stanford University have proved that creative thinking improves while a person is walking and shortly after. So why not try it?

Your brain is the ultimate creative tool. You just have to distract it enough to let it find its way. If you haven't ever written a journal or taken regular walks, it's never too late. You'll be in good company too. Charles Dickens, Virginia Woolf, Beethoven, and Aristotle were all were partial to a purposeless walk, and it certainly worked for them. There are so many proven benefits, I think it's a no-brainer that we all should be doing it.

GET THE JOURNALING HABIT

Ideas for creative walking

1 | NO DIRECTION
Try walking with absolutely
no idea where you're going
(within reason). If you work
full time, do the walking on
the weekend or after work.

2 | KIT
Take a camera or notebook,
perhaps a digital voice
recorder, but use them only
if the mood takes you.

3 | NO PUSHING
Whatever you're feeling or
thinking, don't push those
thoughts aside. Just listen
to them and observe your
surroundings, maybe using
one of your senses to calm
the mind-chatter.

4 | LISTEN
Listen to the squeak of a tree
branch, feel the breeze on

your face, smell the freshly
cut grass. Whatever is there,
go with it.

5 | THREE THINGS
Write down three things
that surprised you on your
walk. How long was it before
you started enjoying yourself?
Did walking help iron out
any issues you may have
had during the day? What
interested you most?

6 | SENSES
Write down the sense you
were most aware of. Did you
stop and build a sculpture
out of sticks on the way, or
did you have to run home
and fashion a pot out of clay?
Perhaps it simply made you
feel relaxed and happy to get
on with your day.

OUT OF OFFICE

CHAPTER 7

OUT OF OFFICE

Walking conversations at work

Alison France | Evosis with
Ruth Williams | Department Store for the Mind

I wear many "hats" and, adorned with one of these, I take the role of a coach within organizations. When listening to the anxiety experienced by Sheila, one of my coaching clients, I was deeply struck by the way she talked about her appraisal discussions:

98

"On the morning of my 'appraisal' I remember waking up abruptly with a tightening in my tummy. The thought of sitting in that small internal room and being eye-to-eye with Sally—my sweet but rather intense line manager—for at least an hour, discussing my performance and aspirations was gut-wrenchingly awful. I wondered, as I lay awake in bed, if those 'appraisal' discussions were a joy for anyone. As I mentally ran through the way my work friends talked about their experiences, I couldn't recall a single one who relished the prospect. At least I wasn't alone in my aversion to this intensity. Pondering the scenario from Sally's perspective, I also couldn't imagine how she might run the thing differently."

This is just one example, which many people will identify with, where the physical setup for the work conversation creates blocks to really doing the thing it claims to be working toward. This situation is very common, particularly in larger organizations, where pressure of work, inadequate office environments, and poor conversations lead to misunderstandings, conflict, and difficult working relationships, which aren't ideal for the company or individuals involved. An appraisal usually aims to create a sense of ease and relaxation, so

" "

STEVE JOBS
WAS A KEEN
ADVOCATE OF
THE WALKING
MEETING, AS
ARE BARACK
OBAMA AND
FACEBOOK
CHIEF MARK
ZUCKERBERG

discussions can be free and frank and a manager can work creatively with their team member to reflect on what they've learned in the past, and imagine and then plan a future that inspires and motivates them both.

Even though Sheila couldn't conceive of a different way for Sally, her manager, to run the meeting, there is an alternative and it's incredibly simple.

Have you guessed? Yes, to simply take the conversation outside and walk together side by side.

WHY TAKE MEETINGS FOR A WALK?

We spend more time sitting than sleeping! It's a scary thought that research is now showing that sitting for more than three hours a day reduces life expectancy. However, we tend to have busy lives, and trying to fit in more time to be active isn't always so easy. Here is a wonderfully simple solution that is spreading across organizations like wildfire—the walking meeting. It's something we can do while working, and the research is showing that not only is it good for our body and mind but it can also make us better at our job!

This is not a new idea by any means. Aristotle was famous for walking around the marketplace with his students as they discussed knotty problems and generated creative solutions. Steve Jobs was a keen advocate of the walking meeting, as are Barack Obama and Facebook chief Mark Zuckerberg—and there are other well-known names that we could add to the list. One thing that many of these people have in common is that they are known to be innovative thinkers—people who challenge the status quo.

The first and maybe biggest barrier to the walking meeting is company culture. However, if tackled right, this need not be an obstacle. Do not be deterred just because there are no walking meetings going on where you work at the moment. You can create movement in this new direction with some simple baby steps, and there is a large weight of solid research to back you up. Here are some of the most fascinating findings that the scientific world has recently unearthed to tempt you into stepping out:

- The 2014 Stanford study by Oppezzo and Schwartz (see page 75) discovered that we are up to 60 percent more creative when walking. Surprisingly, the study found that there was little difference if you were walking on a treadmill inside or meandering along a woodland path outside. It is the physical act of walking that makes the difference. When you consider the vast amounts of money that large organizations invest in encouraging more innovation, then this cheap solution to increasing creativity is a no-brainer.

- The health effects for walking are well documented. Sitting for long periods of time may lead to weight gain, heart disease, raised blood pressure, and even cancer. Research has shown that these negative effects can be flipped through regular walking, in turn saving companies a fortune by reducing staff absence and healthcare costs and by improving performance.

- It's not only the physical-health but also the mental-health benefits of walking that have an astonishing impact. A regular stroll outside is shown to reduce anxiety and depression significantly. One study, conducted by Towers Watson in 2012 and involving a whopping 32,000 employees, found shockingly that 47 percent of them felt that their stress levels were not manageable. When organizations discover this sort of information, they arguably have a duty of care to do something about it (and in some countries are required by law to do so). Just allowing and encouraging people to take walking meetings must be about the cheapest and easiest solution imaginable. Of course, greater access to walking meetings would need to be part of a wider plan when addressing stress at work.

- One study recommends that to have a positive effect on health during the working day, organizations should start by encouraging two hours of standing or walking, with the aim of progressing eventually to four hours. The standing desk might be one way of doing this, but a new way of thinking about meetings surely must be needed to reach the target quota. Since walking has stronger health benefits than standing, then a combination of both is needed.

"" ""

THERE IS
SOMETHING
FUNDAMENTALLY
HUMAN IN
ME THAT
CRAVES
FRESH AIR

- How many of us find ourselves drifting off and daydreaming at some point during the working day? Or maybe procrastinating and not getting down to the job when needed? Walking has been found also to increase attention (Courchesne & Allen, 1997). This is likely to have a positive impact not only on your personal bottom line but also on the company one, as greater attention in employees surely improves the quality and quantity of the work produced.

The body of research is vast, and only a handful of the findings are captured here. The stories we hear of how walking meetings began often involve a tale of insufficient conference rooms and an accidental suggestion to take a stroll instead. Perhaps this is true for your workplace and could be another reason to suggest getting out and about.

THE STORY OF ONE WALKING MEETING

This illustrative tale paints a picture of a more mindful interaction, which inspired very different outcomes than if it had been held in the usual office meeting room.

Lucy was worried: she had become the leader of a mostly male team that she'd been part of for only six months, and she was gradually getting to grips with her new responsibilities. Her boss was starting to put her under pressure to improve performance. She was particularly concerned about George. He was a long-standing member of her team, highly experienced and capable. However, he often got carried away with the technical details of a project, which led to his overengineering solutions. Recently a client had complained that he was constantly missing deadlines, which would impact on the budget. Lucy knew that she needed to schedule a meeting with George but she was worried that he wouldn't take her seriously, partly because she was significantly younger than him, a fact he liked reminding her of regularly as a way of belittling her contributions and undermining her decisions.

Lucy had recently attended a leadership-training course, which had given her some great ideas that might work in this situation. However, she was nervous about trying something new. In her mind, she kept rehearsing the conversation—at best it ended with her not being certain George would take any action, and at worst he stormed out of the meeting. She really didn't want to end up making things even more tense between them, especially since they were going to be spending an evening away, visiting a client the following week.

It was while she was having that thought that she had her idea. At the training course, someone had talked about the benefits of walking meetings. Lucy knew that there was an old, derelict church about 20 minutes' walk away from the bed-and-breakfast where they would be staying. The coastal path to this spot offered some awe-inspiring views. She knew George was a keen walker so she felt optimistic that he would agree to getting some fresh air in the evening. To galvanize herself, she decided to invite George on the walk as soon as she could. A little later in the day, when she noticed him making a cup of tea in the kitchen, she joined him. While navigating kettle, cups, and teabags, Lucy proffered her invitation. She was delighted when George accepted and, even though she was still nervous, she felt hopeful.

The trip arrived. The first day with the client went reasonably well. However, the issue of the slipping timetables had come up. The client had been firm in asking for a revised schedule, being very clear that this must be met. Lucy wasn't surprised and was pleased that this offered a way in to raise the topic of timelines with George. George was feeling rather grumpy and under scrutiny. He was concerned because he felt it took time to produce the high quality of work for which he was known. He didn't like being so restricted by deadlines.

Having spent the day in a stuffy office, both Lucy and George were looking forward to getting some fresh air. After returning to their bed-and-breakfast to get changed, they set off along the path.

Lucy: *"[breathing in] I've been looking forward to this all day—I love this walk. Thanks for joining me."*

George: *"Yes, me too."*

Lucy: *"Have you done much walking lately?"*

George: "Not really. With the winter weather and dark evenings I've not got out as much as I'd like. [pause] I've missed it. You forget how quickly it clears your head."

Lucy: "Yes, especially after an intense day like today!"

George: "Intense is the word!"

Lucy: "You sound concerned..."

George: "Well, yes, they were rather insistent about their deadlines. I'm really worried it will compromise the quality of my work."

Lucy: "Mmm [pause], tell me more."

George: "Well, to get all of the details right, I need to be able to have the freedom to just work until I've finished. With what they're discussing, it looks like I'll have to stop at an arbitrary deadline and just hope it will work."

Lucy: "Yes, I'd be concerned if we were submitting anything to any client and 'hoping' it would work. I guess we need to work on a way we can maintain the quality AND meet the deadline. What would you suggest?"

George: "Well, if I had my way, we'd just tell them to chill out and we'll be ready when we're ready!"

Lucy: "[smiling] I know how you feel, but I don't think we'll get away with that, do you?"

George: "Mmm, no, probably not."

Lucy: "So, any other ideas?"

It took George a while to reply but Lucy felt that staying with the silence was the best choice. She also had the lovely view to look at, and a long pause when out strolling was far easier to hold than it was in a meeting room.

George: *"Well, I suppose I could put together a loose timeline to work to."*

Lucy: *"That would be a real help. [more silence]"*

George: *"And maybe if I found I was getting close to a deadline I could get Saarim to help out."*

Lucy: *"Sounds like a fantastic idea. In fact, I think Saarim would really benefit from working more with you. Maybe you can get him involved soon, so he's up to speed?"*

George: *"The problem with Saarim is that, though he's eager, he has a lot to learn, so it can take me longer to brief him than to do the work myself."*

Lucy: *"Yes, well, do you think that you could factor some of that into your timeline early on?"*

George: *"Mmm, that does sound like it could work..."*

Lucy: *"You sound a bit doubtful still."*

George: *"Yes, I am. It sounds reasonable but I'm not sure it will work in practice."*

Lucy: *"Would it help if I worked with Saarim at the same time to provide some of the support he'll need and make sure he delivers what you want?"*

George: *"That's a great idea, and will save me some time."*

Lucy: *"Wonderful! I think that's the makings of a great solution. Thanks, George!"*

George: *"No problem, I'm glad you suggested this chat. I'm feeling better about the whole thing."*

As Lucy and George continued together, an air of calm, echoed by their surroundings, rested upon them. Lucy was relieved by the easy success of their discussion and was certain that this was the start of a new chapter in their working relationship. Thank goodness, she thought, she hadn't dived in to giving the dreaded formal "feedback" in the office and had tried this out instead. George felt far better about the situation, too. He was definitely going to give their ideas a chance and decided to send a couple of emails to get things moving when they got back that evening.

LEARNING FROM LUCY AND GEORGE

The meeting invitation was offered in advance, the distance was relatively short, and they brought suitable clothes. Fair warning and practical preparations are simple yet key considerations in making the walking meeting a success.

The hierarchy that had been causing stress melted away as the pair strolled. Out of the office, the old roles were quickly forgotten and an easier connection discovered. The rhythm of the pace and the views offered a chance to relax into long silences, which might have been hideously uncomfortable indoors. The silence gave them space to imagine possibilities.

The invitation to walk together felt like a gesture from Lucy to show a little care and compassion for George. They shared something memorable, and they naturally wove appreciation and thanks to each other into their discussion. Just a 40-minute return journey marked a dramatic shift in their relationship.

George made a mental note to send a few emails on return. This is a crucial part of the walking meeting, since you are less likely to be able to make notes while strolling. However, there are apps under development for this specific purpose. It may still be a shame to have the discussion interrupted at all by technology.

We can imagine that Lucy and George may return to the office with happy tales of the walking meeting that began a new movement out of the office. For Lucy, with little to lose and so much to gain, just giving it a try was the best convincer.

There is something fundamentally human in me that craves fresh air and a step away from fluorescent lights and air conditioning. Access to the walking meeting feels like it should be a basic human right, regardless of how the science stacks up.

GET THE OUT-OF-OFFICE HABIT

Ideas for inviting walking at work

1 | "AFTER YOU"
Plan how you will invite your walking partner to join you. Put yourself in their shoes and consider why they might want to join you. Begin your invitation with the benefits for them.

2 | START SMALL
Consider beginning with a short stroll somewhere nearby rather than a long walk into the unknown. You could even suggest going to a café to talk, so it's not even suggested as a "walk."

3 | THE DANCE
Conversations take a rhythm where they begin slowly, build to the main event, then gradually wind down. Let your feet lead the rhythm—slow down, pause, listen, and take time to get there.

4 | INTERWEAVING DISTRACTION
Weave into the conversation observations about the things you pass. Let these rest with your partner and notice how the most random things can open up new thinking.

5 | IMAGINE POSSIBILITIES
Make the most of being outside and the creative thinking it brings. As you stroll, comfortable pauses last longer. It's a great time to share ideas and ask the bigger questions.

6 | FOLLOW UP
Agree together, on your return, what has emerged from your conversation and how you will act, if this is appropriate. Future walks will be more inviting if this one leads to new thinking and action.

ROOTS ON

THE MOVE

ROOTS ON THE MOVE

Healing family dynamics through walking

Gert-Jan de Hoon | Voyage Beyond

This is the story of Kate and Jackson from California—a mother and her 15-year-old son—walking the Camino de Santiago, described in Chapter 4 (*see* page 54). Their route begins in Porto and finishes in Santiago de Compostela: a journey of 155 miles, involving 12 days of walking through the countryside of northern Portugal and, at the halfway point, crossing into Spain. You may wonder what teenage boy would walk this path with his mother? Why were they doing this? And what effect would it have on their relationship? Let me first explain what happens when you walk the Camino, how it works, and why so many people are attracted to this way of slowing their life down and stepping out of overdrive.

The easiest way to explain it is to tell the story of the pilgrims going to Santiago. As people walk, the Camino comes to life; it is as though every story falls from their feet, creating the path. When you follow in their footsteps you have a sense of the stories that have come before you. The Camino is the story of Anika, a Canadian woman who is walking 500 miles with a prosthesis to Santiago; when she was 11 years old, her leg was amputated just above the knee because of bone cancer. It is also the story of Aurel, from Switzerland, who is walking barefoot from the Pyrenees to Santiago. Or the story of Russel, from New Zealand, who is walking with a six-foot wooden cross on his back; he has carved the names of God in 50 languages in the wood. And the story of Josef, who spent a year and a half on the couch doing nothing because of heart failure; he is walking with his mother and girlfriend. Bernard, an artist, is looking for inspiration. Franz, from Germany, attempted suicide 20 years ago; it is his

" "

WHEN PEOPLE
MAKE CHOICES FOR
THEMSELVES, THE
NEW APPROACH
IS LIKELY TO BE
MORE FIRMLY FIXED
IN THEIR FUTURE
THINKING

second time walking. "The Camino is very good for my soul and for my heart," he says. On the journey, you hear extracts and snippets of stories from people. They often talk of facts and events, but the emotion, the journey inside, is with them, with you, and deeply embedded in this path.

WHAT DOES IT MEAN TO BE A PILGRIM?

A pilgrim is more than just a walker on their way to Santiago. A pilgrim lives basically, staying in *albergues*, places only available to pilgrims with a special pass. The accommodation ranges from small places with a few beds to *albergues* with a few hundred beds. Pilgrims are provided with a bunk bed and they bring their own sleeping bag. There are washing facilities and, most of the time, a kitchen. Some places serve a collective evening meal, shared by weary travelers around a long table. A pilgrim normally carries their own stuff on their back, bringing just the essentials. Those who carry too much will shed whatever they don't need, sending it forward to Santiago by mail or leaving it behind for others on the path.

Every day is the same. You wake up in an *albergue*. You get dressed and pack your knapsack. You make breakfast or eat in a café and then set off for another day of walking. You walk to the next village, have a coffee, and something to eat, get some rest at the side of the road, have a picnic, write in your diary and, at the end of the day, arrive at another *albergue*. You find yourself a bed, have a shower, wash your clothes, have a drink, write in your diary again, find out who else has arrived at this place, find somewhere for supper, and go to sleep early. This is the pilgrim's day.

At the same time, every day is also different, as you walk a different part of the Camino; you might find new company or you might walk alone, slowly getting closer to Santiago. You step outside your context and comfort zone and let go of the daily structure of life you are so used to.

FAMILY DYNAMICS ON THE CAMINO

I met Kate and Jackson for the first time in Porto. We had spoken on the phone and over Skype, and they seemed very excited about walking and having me as their guide and Camino coach. When I have previously seen families on the Camino Way, they always seemed to have bonded more deeply through sharing this experience.

On the journey from California to Europe, Kate had lost her phone on the plane. She was very upset about it, as she still had a thousand and one things to do and many emails to send. Yet being free of technology and simply walking is one of the most healing parts of the pilgrimage experience. Without her phone, Kate would feel this fully. She might worry at first about what was happening back in her life at home, but I was looking forward to seeing this worry fade away as she adopted the rhythm of her new life on the path. It seemed as if this had been meant to happen—a sort of synchronicity (a relation between two things happening that can't be explained in a causal way). It was as though the Camino was looking after her very well from the very start.

> "BEING FREE OF TECHNOLOGY
> AND SIMPLY WALKING IS ONE OF
> THE MOST HEALING PARTS OF THE
> PILGRIMAGE EXPERIENCE"

On the first day, we made our way to the cathedral in the center of town. We were lucky as there was a baptism going on, at the end of the Sunday morning service, and we were guests at this old ritual. Here we received our pilgrims' passports and we were ready to start our Camino journey. The next morning, we would be leaving from Matosinhos on the edge of Porto, near the ocean. We would be walking for six days in Portugal and six days in Spain.

JACKSON'S FIRST STEPS

When I met the two at Matosinhos, Jackson's expression was apprehensive and he seemed doubtful and insecure. He was giving me a look as if to say, "What have I got myself into?" He was also challenging any directions, trying to provoke a reaction from me or his mother. His mother gave me a look as if to say, "I don't know what to do about this."

" "

WHAT I HAVE
LEARNED ON
THE CAMINO
IS THAT LIFE
IS ABOUT
PUTTING
ONE FOOT
IN FRONT OF
THE OTHER

Speaking his mind, Jackson said that he was not going to wear his walking boots, that he would be wearing his sneakers all the way. I chose just to observe it all from a distance and let it happen. However, after a little way, Jackson asked if we could stock up on water, as his bottle was empty, and I decided that this was a good time to have a little chat before going any further.

I explained to him that he would be in trouble later if he didn't walk in proper boots. Today it was raining a little but we might have really bad weather and there would be rocky terrain to go through. If he stayed in his sneakers, he was going to have blisters and problems with his feet. He would also need a second pair of shoes to wear in the evening. The choice was his. He took all of this in, eventually saying that he would put on the boots that he was carrying in his pack. Once he had done so, despite the boots being heavier, he seemed a little lighter in his stride.

It was good to let Jackson decide for himself. Having made the decision about the footwear himself, he felt happier about it. When people make choices for themselves, the new approach is likely to be more firmly fixed in their future thinking. My role as coach and guide is to be beside them to support them in their choices. The slow pace and length of time offered by the Camino allow plenty of time for all sorts of choices and learning.

Stocked up on water and food, all walking in our boots, we followed a small path along the coast taking us to the port of Vila do Conde. It was a rainy and windy morning as we left the hectic pace of the city behind us and started our journey, all with our own thoughts, getting used to our packs, and with the ocean to our left. It is moments like this that I cherish the most, when we don't know what to expect and we have everything in front of us, unaware of whom we are going to meet or what we will find out just by putting one foot in front of the other.

Our first days went smoothly, though Kate and Jackson were tired from jet lag. They had just flown in a couple of days previously and had to get used to a time difference of nine hours. Walking is a good medicine for this, too, and time is patient on the Camino.

JACKSON'S STORY

Jackson told me that he had first thought of walking the Camino as a way to solve a deeply troubling problem that was preoccupying him. He had desperately searched for somewhere he could walk. A cousin of his had walked the Camino some years before and had come back with wonderful stories, so he had made up his mind to walk it himself one day. Finishing junior high school seemed a good moment. Walking made him feel happy—a happiness that had eluded him for a while, and that didn't feel like a mask for a depressed soul. Walking also brought him clarity and calmness, and a realization about why he was walking. He was walking for discovery—he wanted to find the cause of his perpetual depression.

In one of the *albergues* Jackson found a guitar and hesitantly asked if he could play. "Of course," the owner said. After an uncomfortable start, feeling very unsure of himself, he became more at ease and the magic started. A Portuguese man began singing, and together they made music that brought the place alive. The atmosphere built up and more pilgrims joined in. Jackson's confidence grew and he seemed more grown-up. I looked across at Kate's ear-to-ear smile and knew that this would be a chapter in their family story remembered for years to come.

"TIME IS PATIENT ON THE CAMINO"

Jackson said, "Initially I thought that walking the Camino with my mom would be weird, that it wouldn't be that fun, but as we began walking I realized it wasn't really all that bad. It felt more like I was friends with her when we walked. We talked and shared the experience of the Camino together. Now we can share the memories of the *albergues*, the faces of the travelers we met, all of us walking to the same place. Both feeling the calmness walking the forest trails filled with eucalyptus. Feeling excited and sad as we walked into Praza Obradoiro in Santiago, overlooked by the cathedral. I didn't know what to expect of the Camino at first, especially the idea of walking it with mom, but I loved it all, loved walking with her, and loved walking the Camino."

" "

THEY LEFT WITH
A GREAT STORY
TO SHARE,
AND A <u>MORE</u>
OPEN WAY OF
<u>COMMUNICATING</u>

Even though Jackson didn't say explicitly to me that he had found the answer to his question about depression, he seemed to find a way through it by being more connected to his mother. I believe the bond they formed was strong enough to survive the journey back home and will provide them with resilience and strength to cope with the stresses and strains of daily life.

KATE'S STORY

On the third morning, Kate was struggling to pack her knapsack, as she had brought too much for this trip. It was too heavy and bulky and she was getting upset. I took some of her load into my pack, and we adjusted hers. She was slowly letting go of physical and emotional baggage and getting into the rhythm of the Camino.

"What is so interesting," said Kate later that day, "is that the desire to do this came from Jackson. He wanted to do this after his eighth-grade graduation. And to be honest, I didn't think I could do it, but I didn't want to let him down, so I went along with it." She smiled when she said this and I saw how moved she was to be sharing this experience with her son.

Toward the end of the trip she reflected on the journey to me. "I have more children, and to spend two weeks with one of them just walking is an amazing experience. Actually, I have not spent this amount of time just with him alone in his life. Walking has made me feel very present with him. To see him in a totally different light, too—opening up, getting more confident, connecting with all these pilgrims. And I realize he is a 15-year-old boy, trying to find himself. It is the best thing that could have happened; such a gift. I haven't seen Jackson more alive than on the Camino. It was such a great experience, meeting all these pilgrims from all over the world. And he saw a different side of me, too, on the last part of the Camino. When we arrived in Santiago I was in such a good space. I was much calmer in the end. Totally in rhythm with the Camino."

Kate has struggled with the mental and physical challenges she has experienced during her life. As we walked she looked healthier, happier and—just like her knapsack—lighter. Her conversations with Jackson seemed easier as the days

" "

THE LIFE-
CHANGING
BIG STORY
IS GREAT
FUN BUT
MOMENTS
BESIDE ONE
ANOTHER IN
RHYTHM CAN
BE CREATED
ON ANY DAY

progressed. They left with a great story to share, and a more open way of communicating that had an ease and humor to it. They had a new respect for each other, something many mothers of teenage boys long for.

"What I have learned on the Camino is that life is about putting one foot in front of the other, like a walking meditation—dealing with your shit, being in your body, and feeling more comfortable in your own skin. The big question is how to incorporate this into my life."

TAKING THE VOYAGE BEYOND

Sometimes the learning that travelers take back to their daily lives is as simple as creating new family stories to share. However, there is something woven through the telling of the story that imparts so much more. You can see it in the way the storytellers finish each other's sentences, the way they laugh at a memory of a tough day together, smile at the thought of a quirky character they encountered or share a pause, remembering a breathtaking story from another traveler that had touched them both.

When family members spend this amount of time pacing slowly beside one another, speaking of whatever comes to mind, then a new connection forms. I believe strongly that you can create a little of the Camino with your family on a shorter walk, too. The life-changing big story is great fun but moments beside one another in rhythm can be created on any day.

GET THE ROOT-MOVING HABIT

Ideas for walking with family and friends

1 | PLAN FREE
When you are taking a longer walk together or with a group, don't plan everything to the second. Leave space for exploring and letting things happen.

2 | SILENCE
When you are walking, you spend a lot of time together, so you can also be quiet with one another. Walk in silence for a period of time and just be with one another.

3 | DIFFERENT EARS
Start listening in a different way. Try to hear what people are really saying. Ask questions in a nonjudgmental way and don't ask questions to find answers. Just help the others tell their story.

4 | TAKE TIME
As Kate says, this was the first time she spent so much time with only one of her children. Taking this time in doing something active together is a key to a better understanding.

4 | SLOW DOWN
Take your time to put your feet in the water or take a nap. Try not to rush to the next stop.

6 | JUST BE
Be with the sun, be with the rain. Be together and expect no more.

BUTTERFLY

BOOTS

BUTTERFLY BOOTS

Taking your worries for a walk

Ruth Williams | Department Store for the Mind

My mind races, my butterflies are dancing to drum and bass, I've forgotten to breathe and everything's getting hotter. At the same time this weird, out-of-body thing happens and I see myself from the outside, looking just like every other poor squashed soul: ambivalent, bored and resigned to daily discomfort. I fix my gaze out toward the blurred brick wall but this does nothing for my nausea. I attempt a self-distraction game of "guess where the shoes are going" with very mild success. This twice-daily trial is, weirdly, both emotionally exhausting and boring; surely there must be an easier way to get to work!

128

Maps have always thrilled me. Maybe I am a bit odd, but, anyway, it's always given my dearest friends a great source of amusement: "Just give Ruth a map and that will keep her happy for hours." Maps to me are a way to explore possibilities and discover hidden treasures (I think there might be a bit of pirate in me somewhere). So, I thought, I'll indulge myself in some map-immersion time and see if I can cover the same route to work on foot.

The map of the London Transport subway (known as the "Tube") is misleading. It disrupts your sense of space, as locations aren't where they seem and the distances shown have little connection with the real gaps between stations. Massively relieved, I realized that the hideous subway commute was pretty short in real terms. It looked like, just maybe, the squash, stink, and panic could be avoided without needing to give it all up to live on a remote country farm. No disrespect intended to that choice of life, it's just that I'm a city girl at heart and I think my idealistic image of "the good life" may be a tad misguided.

" "

THE WORKING DAY,
WHICH WASN'T
ALWAYS EASY,
FELT LIGHTER AND
MORE DOABLE

THE FIRST LACING OF THE BOOTS

Nothing ventured, nothing gained and all that. I popped a few weather-ready items into a backpack along with laptop and office shoes. Lacing up my boots, I set off extra early, in case of unexpected eventualities. The route took me almost entirely along the Thames Path, a mostly muddy footpath snaking along beside the mighty Thames River.

That first walk was breathtaking. The quiet, beautiful detail and soothing calm of being near the water were wonderful, yet they were more than matched in impact by the huge wave of relief I felt at having found a way out of the daily panic. The working day, which wasn't always easy, felt lighter and more doable. I felt armed with an invisible "happy feet mood" shield. The less-than-subtle jibes of a particularly glam colleague seemed ridiculous and funny, the loosely veiled sexism of the IT team floated high over my happy head, and the incoherent babbling of our leader felt a little endearing. Added to all this, I'd burned off a few extra calories and had more pennies in my wallet. A treat was in order and a meal out at lunchtime filled that role. Day One, the on-foot option turned out to be a no-brainer!

So here I was—I guess like many others, with what was at the time an undiagnosed anxiety disorder—having found a simple way out. I started delving into the research to discover what was happening to my body and brain. Why did this simple change in my commute (which had actually saved me time) have such an unexpectedly big impact? Here are some of the things I discovered.

OUTING THE NASTIES

Exercise helps to reduce the levels of a hormone called cortisol, which is created in the body in response to stress and low blood-sugar levels. It appears to switch off certain nonessential functions so the body can either deal with the low blood sugar or focus on getting us out of danger. Like all animals, we need this mechanism to give our body a boost when we have to escape from life-threatening risks.

However, most of us don't encounter too many hungry lions or grizzly bears in the city, so our stress-management system can become a bit disrupted by the subtler threats we encounter during modern urban life. Stress has the effect of making us feel as though we are in a strange, low-level, near-constant state of danger, so the cortisol just builds up. This seems to be an all-too-common part of crazy city busyness.

"MOST OF US DON'T ENCOUNTER TOO MANY HUNGRY LIONS OR GRIZZLY BEARS IN THE CITY, SO OUR STRESS-MANAGEMENT SYSTEM CAN BECOME A BIT DISRUPTED"

Left alone, elevated cortisol levels can do some seriously nasty stuff, including making bones weaker, stopping the brain from doing its best job, disrupting sleep, making muscles weaker, increasing blood pressure, increasing the time it takes to get over coughs and colds, increasing body fat...the list goes on, to a seriously scary length. So excess cortisol, a common product of busy city life, can't be left hanging around creating havoc without consequences. What a relief that something as simple as changing the commute to more of a walk can go a good way toward helping.

131

DROPPING THE DEFENSES

The other part of this first experience of walking to work that really intrigued me was how differently I felt about other people in the office. These are people who, if I'm perfectly honest, I would not have chosen to spend time with if I didn't have to work with them. However, on this new "walking day" I felt warmer to them, almost as though I could be tempted to share (rather than avoid) an invitation for a drink after work. In truth, I felt less defensive. I guess it makes sense that if my brain has spent 45 minutes on the London Underground feeling scared, then some ghost of that emotion will be lurking in my head, leaving me with a sensation that danger is imminent. This would obviously lead to a bit of an irrational defensive reaction. So I'm potentially freed from some of that, too.

" "

WE KNOW THAT
THE BRAIN
SHAPES ITSELF
BASED ON WHAT
IT EXPERIENCES
HABITUALLY

We know that the brain shapes itself based on what it experiences habitually. Regular bouts of fear will strengthen the part of the brain that serves this function, meaning that my thinking will slip into this state of anxiety easily as the "fear area" gets stronger. Therefore it seems likely that the more I walk, the less cortisol will swill around my system, the less scared I will feel, the less defensive I will become and the friendlier I may be. The bit of the brain benefiting from the morning exercise will be the bit that controls happiness and positivity, so this will get stronger and the part of the brain controlling fear will weaken. This sounds brilliant and is probably good for work, too, because if I want to spend more time with my colleagues, and be a little more open with them, then I'm likely to feel happier and perhaps do a better job.

FEELING LIKE AN IMPOSTOR

Almost all of us get the sensation at some time in our life that we are an impostor in our own job/relationships/clubs and that at any point someone is going to discover our true self and out us to the wide-eyed public. Here are the roots of mine.

I grew up in a fairly affluent middle-class area, the daughter of the only parents on the street with no high school diploma, let alone a university degree, which many of the other parents possessed. We could afford our spot on the sunnier side of town because my parents had bought a very dilapidated house and my dad used his amazing home-renovation skills to convert it over 20 years. I did well at school, then later at university. Many of my friends also flourished at school and university, so I spent my time generally with people whose families were different from mine. The sense of being something of an impostor started from an early age.

As I moved up in the world of work, I would often find myself surrounded by people who'd mostly been educated at private schools and who would ask what school I had attended. I realized after a while that, in certain circles, this was a normal question to establish your background credentials (how good was the private school you attended and did we share connections there?) rather than an invitation for a rundown of shocking stories from your high school (of which I had many). The reason for the often glazed eyes, slow turning away from me and gradual closing of conversations, following my high-school shock stories, gradually became clear. I switched my answer to a more palatable "nowhere too familiar" followed by a distraction to move toward university name-dropping, where I had a little more to offer.

All of this left me feeling less than my honest self and even more of an impostor. The dormant, and then not-so-dormant, anxiety swirled around inside my head, and that evil squash-and-squeeze of a commute heightened it all to nerve-racking proportions. However, after my morning explorations in boots, the impostor feelings and anxiety had dramatically faded and I felt able to be a little more of my truer self. So, could the walk have changed this thinking, too?

> "AFTER MY MORNING EXPLORATIONS IN BOOTS, THE IMPOSTOR FEELINGS AND ANXIETY HAD DRAMATICALLY FADED AND I FELT ABLE TO BE A LITTLE MORE OF MY TRUER SELF"

ANYTHING GOES

Being outside in nature or public spaces, we see it all. Instead of the unspoken, ever-changing, detailed rules of corporate life, there is a general acceptance that pretty much anything goes. People of all kinds can be found along the river. Some live here on wonderfully eccentric houseboats, others wake from a night of restless sleep beneath a drafty bridge, and still others sip coffee on the tiny balconies of incredibly expensive contemporary waterside developments, yet all share this space.

There is something soothing to a person who has the impostor syndrome when they witness, through their own eyes, how dramatically different people are, and see real diversity in action. The closer and more regular our encounters with these differences, the greater the potential for seeing similarities, too. They seem to say "that's OK" and that we will all find our own ways of seeing, being, and surviving, with or without the judgment of others.

What's more, walking allows the brain to be far more creative. We have free space to imagine, and our feet beat a rhythm that has a meditative quality. This means that what we see and experience as we stroll drifts into our conscious and subconscious mind, shaping our daydreams and the direction of our mental wanderings. If we are only walking, smartphones and headphones switched off, then our eyes and mind have space to absorb and contemplate those details.

So, here I am seeing a rich multitude of life as it begins its city day, and I realize that I, too, can be different. As myself, I am part of the beauty that diversity brings to the city. In fact, I feel more than this. I feel that my smile, steps, and obvious enjoyment of the space bring something that makes me, as I am right now, a worthwhile being. The most perfect medicine for a sufferer of the impostor syndrome is easy access to an experience that gives license to be one's self. To be able to access this daily, even twice daily, was a complete tonic.

AFTER THE FIRST DAY

We can choose the habits we form. We need them just as all animals do, and our habits will define who we are. This walk had such an astounding impact on me that it easily became a habit. The weather was something I started to worry a little about but I made a firm decision that, even though I had started in summer, any rain or snow would not weaken my resolve.

To my amazement, I found that adverse weather could have an even brighter impact. There was something about the commitment to looking after one's self that walking in the rain showed. The benefit to my inner being was worth the temporary discomfort to my outer being, and, in fact, my outer being actually didn't mind as much as I thought it might. Something of the pioneering spirit was awakened in me when I could proudly proclaim to my fellow office-dwellers that, yes, I had walked all the way to work in this weather. Now feeling different seemed like a personal badge of honor and, I hoped, could be something of an inspiration for others to do the same.

Sharing stories of moments of anxiety, particularly at work, can be difficult. However, whenever I have made the brave step to do this, people have surprised me by reciprocating and sharing how their own moments of doubt

" "

THE BENEFIT
TO MY INNER
BEING WAS
WORTH THE
TEMPORARY
DISCOMFORT TO
MY OUTER BEING

or anxiety affect them. The story of my walking commute was an easy one to tell because I could focus on what I did to heal those butterflies in my stomach. Imagine how many untold stories of ways to cope other people have stored away in their mind's treasure chest. If we take the first step and start these conversations, then maybe we can unlock the secrets, learn from one another, and try out a few new, helpful habits.

The winter came and snow fell. I wondered if I could still make it. Would the footpath be too slippery? Would I slide unnoticed into icy water? Probably not, so with extra time allowed and extra woolens adorned, I went for it! The sights were so beautiful. The morning light, the classic red of the robin's breast against the white snow, and the postcard-perfect puffs of white wood-burner smoke billowing from the houseboats, all amid the hush that snowfall brings, were astounding. My feet did not fail me, unlike most of the rest of the city's public transit system that day, so I arrived at work happy and refreshed. I had a lovely story to tell friends, clients, and strangers I met that day, hopefully one that inspired and encouraged others to free the butterflies, lace up the boots, and seek an alternative habit to start the day.

GET THE BUTTERFLY-BOOTS HABIT

Ideas for walking away from anxiety

1 | TUNE IN!

How does your body send you messages? What might those butterflies in the stomach, aches in the back, unexplained tiredness, or throbbing temples be trying to tell you? Could you listen a little more closely?

2 | TAKE CONTROL

Small, even tiny, steps remind you that you can get control back, and they can help you break out rather than spiral in. Can you find a chance to step outside when anxiety sets in, even if it is just for a minute?

3 | GROW POSITIVE

Take the first tiny step and notice how it feels. Can you find a time to do it again? Can you make it slightly longer or take it slightly farther this time? Notice how the second outing feels, inside and out.

4 | HABIT KIT

Can an object help you to make the positive step stick? Maybe a bracelet to flick to remind you to step outside, a hat to wear to tell yourself "I'm putting on the walking me," or new walking boots to lace up?

5 | ALL SEASONS

How might you be ready to keep the outside habit going, whatever the weather? What extra gear might you need? What sort of thinking will keep you strolling, breathing, and noticing? Prepare the mind, too.

6 | SHARE

Can you spot an opportunity to share your story? One telling at a time, we can change how people feel about talking about their mental health. How might you tip things in a good direction?

BACKWARD

BINOCULARS

BACKWARD
BINOCULARS

Walk to find perspective

Ruth Williams | Department Store for the Mind

My two-year-old loves to pick up binoculars and look through them the other way around. I had to try it to see the attraction. The world is small and focused. It's also much easier to see when you look into something bigger (the large end) to find something smaller. We can see the detail of a small area when it has a neat circular frame. A little like a magnifying glass, the backward binoculars draw the eye to the detail of an area right in front of us. We get to see the familiar from a new perspective without the distraction of any surrounding visual information.

142

Children often naturally do the easier thing, without any obvious conscious consideration. They just get on with it. For most, their limited life-experience leaves them free of the fear of past failure or the limitations of imagined social expectation. They just see and react to the immediate situation as it is, then they experiment until they find something that interests or amuses them. So binoculars, a favorite piece of hiker's gear for discovering faraway curiosities hidden to the naked eye, also become a way into revealing the detail of the close and familiar.

The idea that what we see can shape how our mind works fascinates me. I live by the sea and I never tire of looking out to the horizon and seeing the water meet the sky, which must be one of the most popular images all over the world for communicating serenity. I watch my boys when we go to the beach, and

" "

TAKE ALL
THE ADVICE
AND IDEAS YOU
ENCOUNTER, THEN
FORGET THEM,
LISTEN TO YOUR
INSTINCT, AND
EXPERIMENT

they slow down, wander, explore, discover, and become calm and gently playful. But what happens in our body and brain when we are experiencing the inner peace that a quiet beach can bring?

SPACE TO THINK

So far in this book we have focused on how walking, particularly outside, can provide a sense of calm and make focusing a little easier. Being on a peaceful beach has a similar effect, because its calming effect helps us quieten the inner chatter of our mind, reducing emotional distractions. At the same time, it reduces the physical distractions that come from the stimulation of the senses. When all there is on offer to our eyes is the sea and the sky, when all we feel is the wind and sun on our skin, when all we hear is the rhythm of the waves, and when all we smell is the sea, there is less to distract us. As a result, the mind is freer to consider inner thoughts. We simply have more mental resources available and are more likely to be able to find a way through any problems.

"BY LOOKING AT MOUNTAINS, THE MOUNTAINS INSIDE US ACTUALLY BECOME MOLEHILLS!"

Of course we will not always have a quiet beach nearby but we may still be able to make choices about the things we allow to distract our senses. Creating spaces with low levels of sensory stimulation, where you can focus on thinking during your day-to-day life, can give you a mental recharge. So much of everyday urban life is just overwhelming our senses, and we need to fight back a little to keep our sanity and take care of ourselves. Each of us is a wonderfully complex and unique array of quirks and qualities. The trick is to take all the advice and ideas you encounter, then forget them, listen to your instinct, and experiment. Keep playing with situations and ideas, locations, and thoughts until you find the space that works for you. If I want to write, I find sitting in my kitchen looking out onto the garden, with the steady whir of the dishwasher in the background, to be calming. If I have a knotty question to consider, then a walk around the park for as little as ten minutes can spark a lightbulb moment and begin the journey in a new direction.

A SENSE OF AWE

There's something else about walking outside that excites me. It's that sensation I feel when I notice something so beautiful it makes me feel small, sometimes described as a sense of awe. Feeling moments of awe is healing. Here are a few ways this works:

- The sensation is (at least momentarily) all-encompassing. There's no space for anything else in our head, so the awe-inspiring thing takes over. Our worries about the past and future melt away and we are filled with a feeling of awe in the now. This is being present and it's such a relief to feel it.

- We feel small. Humbled sometimes. Our concerns shrink, reflected in the mirror of the expansiveness and beauty of something that is far bigger than we are. By looking at mountains, the mountains inside us actually become molehills!

- We feel connected to something bigger and have a sense of being part of that. Research shows that our focus shifts from being concerned with what's going on for ourselves to what's happening with others and the world around us. It's a break from worrying about our own inner chatter, which we are zoning out in favor of a more encouraging outside noise, one of beauty and hope.

Taking time to look at whatever inspires in you a sense of awe will naturally do all this, which is, in fact, another explanation for why walking can have such a powerful effect on us. We know that putting one foot in front of the other awakens greater creativity, we know that exercise clears out chemicals in the body that increase stress, and now we also know that feeling inspired is a dramatic mood-changer on its own. When we walk we can do all of this simultaneously. Just imagine how the creativity and the sensations of awe must work together in our mind. It's no wonder that artists, writers, and so many great thinkers walk to access their best selves.

" "

OUR CONCERNS
SHRINK, REFLECTED
IN THE MIRROR OF
THE EXPANSIVENESS
AND BEAUTY OF
SOMETHING THAT
IS FAR BIGGER
THAN WE ARE

MOUNT RINJANI, LOMBOK, INDONESIA

When I was 22, in the late 1990s, I found myself on the island of Lombok in Indonesia. On our trip, we were making up our adventure as we went, based on tips from locals and passing travelers. The island of Lombok had come up repeatedly, described as somewhere freer of tourists than its neighbor Bali. Mount Rinjani, Indonesia's second-highest volcano, offering a climb to 12,224 feet above sea level to look down on its molten smoking heart, was a would-be adventurer's temptation we could not resist. We gathered, enthused, and maybe even cajoled travelers we had befriended in hostels on the journey there, until we had a little group. Then we selected a guide, who recruited two sherpas, and we were set to leave within a couple of days.

Here's the composition of our group. My super-athletic brother, who regularly went off in the morning for a run of 5 to 10 miles. Penny, who had recently cycled across the Pyrenees and possessed an upbeat passion for activity that both inspired and slightly annoyed me. Kat, whose home was in mountains on the Austrian–German border, where she ran across the peaks for fun and competition. Dylan, who didn't so much walk as drift in a meditative state, but still at quite a pace, and had spent the last six months walking in the Australian outback; although very calming to be around, he said very little. Then there was me. It didn't really occur to me that I might struggle to keep up with this group. I was fairly active without being athletic. I cycled to get around and loved to dance. I could go out clubbing and dance energetically till 2 A.M. and beyond. I intermittently attended yoga classes. My diet could have been healthier, and I kept trying to give up cigarettes but remained a guilty social smoker.

The sherpas walked in flip-flops and carried cooking equipment, food, and tents. They moved with an incredible lightness and regularly zipped off ahead. They waited, chatting on a convenient rock, while our little group and guide caught up. After Day One I was tired, and by Day Three tears streamed down my face as I paced through the pain in my muscles and feet, determined not to be beaten by my brother. The scenery and the experience were amazing but what happened to me here was a personal evaluation of the choices I was making in my life. I was younger than almost everyone else in the group but they were far fitter and stronger. I could tell stories of parties and wild escapes from city dangers, and laugh till dawn about taking the easy option. Maybe for the first time, I saw this life in a new light and I wanted to write something different for my future.

MENTAL PATHWAYS

As the brain grows, even before we are born, its nerve cells, called neurons, form millions of connections based on such factors as the things we observe with our senses, the choices we make, and the consequences of those choices. These neural connections become the mental pathways the mind walks along each day. The mental pathways walked more frequently become easier to find and easier to follow, and so are increasingly popular routes.

This phenomenon is similar to the pathways we find weaving through popular woodlands, where the well used routes are easiest to navigate and are the ones we are most likely to follow. If we want to take a new direction down a path far less traveled, it requires some conscious attention. We may need to muster a will to make a choice that might feel different and slightly scary. It may take us through unfamiliar territory where the way ahead is less clear. We then need to stick to it, even when others don't appear to be joining us on our path.

"IF WE WANT TO TAKE A NEW
DIRECTION DOWN A PATH FAR
LESS TRAVELED, IT REQUIRES
SOME CONSCIOUS ATTENTION"

What's amazing about the brain, though, is how flexibly and quickly it will adapt to a new neural pathway. Before long, with a little continued conscious effort, the old, no-longer-used path becomes overgrown, like a forest absorbing the footprints of years back into the earth. Our new route becomes a habit and we slip easily into it, almost forgetting there was ever another way to go. Imagining the creation of new pathways through the mind, just as we would discover and make familiar newly discovered paths through a woodland walk, is something I find really helpful in understanding how the brain works.

" "

THIS

MEANT

TO

ME

THAT,

ALONE,

WE

WERE

ALL

ONE

The stark and painful experience of Mount Rinjani began a new chapter in my thinking. As the muscle aches subsided, the old pathways in my mind—the old habits—seemed to lead to somewhere less glitzy and fun than I'd previously imagined. During the following months, as I continued on my travels, I mulled it over and searched for a new way to imagine the shape that the rest of my twenties might take.

Looking back now to that time, I can see I was searching through my mental forest to discover the intersecting paths that needed remapping. It was easier to concentrate on one or two intersections rather than try to control and remap the whole thing. After all, if I could work out a better route at these points, chances were that the rest would fall into place.

> "I WAS SEARCHING THROUGH
> MY MENTAL FOREST TO DISCOVER
> THE INTERSECTING PATHS THAT
> NEEDED REMAPPING"

In Australia, my brother and I went our separate ways and later in the same month I met Susanne. We traveled together for the next year exploring the Australian outback, the islands of New Zealand, Fiji, and America. For six months of this period we drove in a turquoise campervan around Australia, spending our nights in the national parks and our days walking in the most beautiful, spacious, awe-inspiring places I had ever seen.

Susanne is gentle, listens endlessly without passing comment, loves to laugh with you at the quirky and seemingly absurd, and will sit beside you in silence for longer than anyone else I have ever met. Walking side by side together, we realized how free we felt without the advice or judgments of anyone else.

There was a time in Australia's Blue Mountains, as we sat on a high viewpoint to rest, looking over the blue haze of the eucalyptus forest, that I noticed just how governed my choices had been by what I had perceived as others' expectations. This was the intersection in my mind-forest that needed remapping. I wanted to be as free from thinking about how others are judging me as I felt when in a location like this.

There is something about the beauty and brutality of nature that liberates you from others' judgments.

ALONE OR ALL ONE?

Another thing the walking, talking, and silence helped me to realize is how afraid I had been of being alone. As this idea flitted in and out of my thinking, I can remember becoming fascinated with something I noted in my journal about the word "alone." I wrote about it being the combination, the coming together of the word "all" and the word "one." This meant to me that, alone, we were all one. There was something deliciously liberating about this new way of thinking about being alone. This was the second intersection in my mind-forest that I began to remap. I didn't consciously write more, but on this trip I did start to feel confident about traveling alone. Susanne and I split up for weeks at a time in New Zealand and then met again at intervals. I more than coped and it was wonderful. It was the start of something.

Choosing to walk is choosing to take care of yourself. In a myriad of near magical ways, it opens the mind's rustiest gates with well oiled ease to give license to happy roaming. We each deserve a little time with ourselves to speak freely and cease the inner chatter, so we may rest beside ourselves and breathe. Just as the backward binoculars create a new perspective when we focus through something big to discover the detail of something smaller, so may we discover something significant and awe-inspiring within ourselves when we notice the beauty in the detail.

GET THE BINOCULARS HABIT

Ideas for playing with perspectives

1 | NEW VIEW

When might you take a moment to play with perception the way a child does? What happens when you add a frame or zoom in and out of the details contained within the things you observe? Just notice.

2 | LESS STIMULATION

On your average day, how much information are your senses processing? How might you lessen the load a little? How does it feel when you do? Are there ways to do this more regularly?

3 | AWE-SPOTTING

A quiet beach alone is wonderful but awe is on offer everywhere. Can you discover a sense of wonder in three things each day? Like a detective, can you find the smallest detail possible?

4 | MIND-FOREST

Where are the well trodden paths in your mind? What triggers act as signposts along the way? What paths work for you? Which ones lead you offtrack? Could you draw a map of them?

5 | REMAPPING

Can you detect any intersections in your mind-forest where a different route could work out for you? What might help you push through and make this overgrown section a well trodden route?

6 | SELF-CARE

When is the time in your day that you reflect? How could you create more of these moments? What do you do with this time? What might help you spend it noticing your own beautiful details?

REFERENCES, RESOURCES, AND CREDITS

REFERENCES

Chapter 2

Austen, Jane (2000) *Emma*. Ware, Wordsworth Classics

Barrie, J. M. (2015) *Peter Pan*. London, Harper Collins

Chaucer, Geoffrey (2002) *The Canterbury Tales—New Edition*. London, Bibliophile Books

Johnstone, Keith (2007) *Impro: Improvisation and the Theatre*. London, Bloomsbury

Shakespeare, William (1992) *A Midsummer Night's Dream*. Ware, Wordsworth Classics

Shakespeare, William (2017) *King Lear*. Ware, Wordsworth Classics

Thomassen, Bjorn (2014) *Liminality and the Modern: Living Through the In-Between*. London, Ashgate Publishing

Chapter 3

Adventure Clubs for Kids. (accessed March 15, 2017). www.theoutdoorsproject.co.uk

Oxford Living Dictionaries. (accessed 1 April 2017) English definition of "nature." en.oxforddictionaries.com/definition/nature

Saraswati, Swami Niranjanananda (2012) *Yoga in Daily Life*. India, Yoga Publications Trust

Vagnozzi, Barbara (2007) *Jack and the Beanstalk* (Flip-Up Fairy Tales), Swindon, Child's Play (International) Ltd.

Chapter 4

Gerald, Kelly (2012) *Camino de Santiago—Practical Preparation and Background: Volume 1*. CreateSpace Independent Publishing Platform

Chapter 5

Collins Dictionaries. (accessed March 28, 2017) English translation of "*inspirare.*" www.collinsdictionary.com/dictionary/italian-english/inspirare

Oppezzo, M. and Schwartz, D. L. (2014) "Give Your Ideas Some Legs: The Positive Effect of Walking on Creative Thinking." In: *Journal of Experimental Psychology: Learning, Memory, and Cognition*, 40, 1142–52.

Chapter 6

Beard, Mary (accessed June 13, 2014) "Mary Beard's Greece: A Walk on the Wise Side." The Guardian online. www.theguardian.com/travel/2014/jun/13/mary-beard-walking-aristotle-trail-greece-halkidiki

Bergland, Christopher (accessed January 23, 2013) "Cortisol—Why the Stress Hormone is Public Enemy Number 1." *Psychology Today* online. www.psychologytoday.com/blog/the-athletes-way/201301/cortisol-why-the-stress-hormone-is-public-enemy-no-1

Cameron, Julia (1995) *The Artist's Way: A Course in Discovering and Recovering Your Creative Self.* London, Pan Books

Courchesne, E. and Allen, G. (1997) "Prediction and Preparation, Fundamental Functions of the Cerebellum." In: *Learning & Memory*, 4(1), 1–35

Goldsworthy, Andy (2008) *Time.* London, Thames & Hudson

Higgins, Charlotte (accessed June 15, 2012). "Richard Long: 'It was the swinging 60s. To be walking lines in fields was a bit different'." *The Guardian* online. www.theguardian.com/artanddesign/2012/jun/15/richard-long-swinging-60s-interview

Pennebaker, James W. (2010) *Writing to Heal: A Guided Journal for Recovering from Trauma and Emotional Upheaval.* Oakland, New Harbinger Publications

Robinson, Lawrence et al. (accessed April 2017) "Laughter is the Best Medicine—The Health Benefits of Humor and Laughter." Helpguide. org. www.helpguide.org/articles/emotional-health/laughter-is-the-best-medicine.htm

Wax, Ruby (2016) *A Mindfulness Guide for the Frazzled.* London, Penguin

Chapter 7

Berkowitz, Joe. (accessed August 17, 2015) "Literally Walking Toward Better Ideas: The Creative Habits of Demetri Martin." *Fast Company* online. www.fastcocreate. com/3049900/literally-walking-toward-better-ideas-the-creative-habits-of-demetri-martin

Parker, Brandy and McCammon, Lodge (accessed June 2015) "Walking Meetings: The Research on Why We Should 'Walk and Talk'." flipthemeeting.com/wp-content/uploads/2015/04/WalkTalk-Research.pdf

Peck, Emily (accessed April 9, 2015) "Why Walking Meetings Can Be Better than Sitting Meetings." *Huffington Post* online. www.huffingtonpost.com/2015/04/09/walking-meetings-at-linke_n_7035258.html

Teychenne, M., Costigan, S. A., and Parker, K. (2015) "The Association Between Sedentary Behaviour and Risk of Anxiety: A Systematic Review." In: *BMC Public Health*, 15, 1–8

Towers Watson. (accessed April 9, 2012) "2012 Global Workforce Study, Engagement at Risk: Driving Strong Performance in a Volatile Global Environment." www.towerswatson.com/Insights/IC-Types/Survey-ResearchResults/2012/07/2012-Towers-Watson-Global-Workforce-Study

Chapter 9

Graden, John (2008) *The Impostor Syndrome: How to Replace Self-Doubt with Self-Confidence and Train Your Brain for Success.* Xlibris Corp.

Chapter 10

Bergland, Christopher (accessed May 20, 2015) "The Power of Awe: A Sense of Wonder Promotes Loving-Kindness." *Psychology Today* online. www.psychologytoday.com/blog/the-athletes-way/201505/the-power-awe-sense-wonder-promotes-loving-kindness

Gilson, Nicholas et al (2008) "Experiences of Route and Task-Based Walking in a University Community: Qualitative Perspectives in a Randomized Control Trial." In: *Journal of Physical Activity and Health.* 5(1), 176–82

RESOURCES

Websites

Places to find a walking partner in the United States.

www2.ava.org/
www.womenwalking.net

Books

Germer, Christopher K. (2009) *The Mindful Path to Self-Compassion.* New York: The Guilford Press

Neff, Kristin. (2011) *Self Compassion: Stop Beating Yourself Up and Leave Insecurity Behind.* London: Hodder & Stoughton

CREDITS

Thank you to our talented authors, artists, and designers who share our passion for the power of strolling outdoors:

Louise Ellaway
London-based writer and musician who is committed to applying her many talents to achieving positive social change.

John-Paul Flintoff—www.flintoff.org
and www.speaklisten.co.uk
Writer, performer, and coach who helps organizations and individuals change the world, one conversation at a time.

Kate Peers—madabouttheboys.net
Writer, frequent contributor to *Metro* online, and published author in *The Mother Book* by Selfish Mother.

Gert-Jan de Hoon—www.voyagebeyond.org
An accomplished transformational coach, speaker, Camino guide, and author of *A Pilgrimage to Santiago*.

Clare Barry—www.urbancuriosity.org
Founder of Urban Curiosity, a wellness and creativity company that helps busy people slow down and see things differently.

Antonia Thompson—
www.antoniathompson.uk
Brighton-based artist with a media background (former editor at *The Huffington Post*, AOL, Sky, and ITV).

Alison France—www.evosis.co.uk
Organization and leadership specialist and psychologist with a love for the calm of yoga and the exhilaration of motorbike riding.

Ruth Williams—
www.deptstoreforthemind.com
Business psychologist and director at Department Store for the Mind.

Photography: Libi Pedder—
www.libipedder.com
Photographer of images that resonate and convey—in an immediate sense—an emotion, an atmosphere, or a vulnerability revealed.

Illustration: Alexandra Ethell—
www.theearlyhours.com.au
Melbourne-based graphic designer who makes magic happen in the early hours.

Design: Supafrank Design—
www.supafrank.com
Katie Steel and Jo Raynsford at Supafrank dig deep enough to unearth the spark, hook, or story, weaving this through their work with expert subtlety.

159